T0352407

Egypt in Flux

Egypt in Flux

Essays on an Unfinished Revolution

ADEL ISKANDAR

The American University in Cairo Press
Cairo New York

First published in 2013 by
The American University in Cairo Press
113 Sharia Kasr el Aini, Cairo, Egypt
420 Fifth Avenue, New York, NY 10018
www.aucpress.com

"Geddo and Messianic Football," "On Marina and Chávez," "The Simulacra of Religious Intolerance," "Learning to Mourn with the Poles," "Never Say No to the Panda," "Best in Show," "The Hegemony of Sharks," "The End of Illegitimacy," "Coptic Exodus from Disneyland," "Ablaze the Body Politic," "Dared to Defy," "On Constitutional Reform," "Liberating the Media," "Who's Your Daddy?" "The Three-Horned Bull," "The Conscientious Objectors," "Morsi's Debts," "A Seven A," "Patron Saints," "New Face," "Lemons and Raisins," and "Blood Ballots" were previously published in *Egypt Independent*. Versions of "Reclaiming Silence" were previously published in *Egypt Independent* and the *Huffington Post*. "The Gravity of Pharaohs" was previously published in the *Huffington Post* and *Egypt Independent*. "The Ax-bearers" was previously published under the title "The *Baltageya*" in *Egypt Independent*. "After Maspero" was previously published under the title "Muslim, Christian—One Hand!" in the book *Demanding Dignity*, edited by Maytha Alhassan and Ahmed Shihab-Eldin (Ashland, Ore.: White Cloud Press, 2012). "Year of the Ostrich" and "A Nation Derailed" were previously published in *Jadaliyya*. "Tragedy and Farce" was previously published under the title "Egypt's Shooting of an Elephant" in *Egypt Independent*. "Media Forms" was previously published under the title "Watching the Demise of Journalistic Form" in *Egypt Independent*. All reproduced by permission.

Dar el Kutub No. 14035/12
ISBN 978 977 416 596 2

Dar el Kutub Cataloging-in-Publication Data

Iskandar, Adel
    Egypt in Flux: Essays on an Unfinished Revolution / Adel Iskandar.—Cairo: The American University in Cairo Press, 2013.
       p. cm.
       ISBN 978 977 416 596 2
       1. Egypt – History
       962

1 2 3 4 5   17 16 15 14 13

Designed by Jon W. Stoy
Printed in Egypt

To the motorcycle riders who in November 2011 on Muhammad Mahmud Street shuttled the injured to hospitals and the dead to morgues as battles raged between revolutionaries and the regime. Others were busy campaigning for elections.

And to those revolutionaries who prevented anyone with a university degree from accessing the front lines so they can live on to rebuild the country. They are the guardians of the revolution, not those in the corridors of power nor those who speak in their name.

For Sophia, who arrived in a changing world.

Contents

Acknowledgments

This book would not be possible had it not been for the sacrifices of ordinary people in Bahrain, Egypt, Jordan, Libya, Morocco, Saudi Arabia, Tunisia, Yemen, and everywhere else in the Arab world where the call for freedom reverberated in the streets. It is easy to be either cynical and jaded or overly optimistic and delusional about the progress of the uprisings in general and the Egyptian revolution specifically. However, history offers us the context we need to comprehend the present. To parse through this past and disentangle it, I am indebted to my mentor, who to my fortune is also my father, Dr. Talaat Iskandar Farag. A true visionary, a student leader during the pre-1952 revolutionary protest movement at Ibrahim Pasha University (now Ain Shams University), and a graduate of the college's first class of medicine, he was embroiled in Egypt's political and intellectual life from his teens. He worked at *Rose al-Yusuf* under Ihsan Abd al-Quddus, at the Physicians' Syndicate, and in Yemen, Libya, Kuwait, and most recently in Canada. He has been my entry point into a lost generation of pioneers—a living archive of Egypt's contemporary history and long freedom struggle. It was through him that I met and befriended the late veteran journalist Muhammad Ouda, the late literary giant Khairy Shalaby, pioneer cartoonist Ahmed Toughan, and many others. It was through him that I conversed with fabled rebel Sa'd Zaghlul Fouad and learned about President Anwar al-Sadat's pre-revolutionary days from Sadat's most intimate friends. I came to understand why the 1950s were a time of phenomenal ferment, with a sharp resemblance to our generation's struggle. I came to understand how the Free Officers eventually cannibalized their own children. Everyone was suppressed, from the Marxists to the Islamists, all in the name of unity and stability. As Egyptian politics got murky and questionable, my father abandoned it all and redirected his energy toward his vocation. When asked about this past, he would assertively and dismissively declare, "I am a doctor, D-O-C-T-O-R, a DOCTOR. That is all!" He tried to efface or erase the past either as a defense mechanism or an attempt at some semblance of normalcy. Now in his early eighties, he has outlived many of his contemporaries, his compatriots, his friends, their collective amnesia, the fading archives, and now even that most fearsome state apparatus. Listening to him reflect about his sixty-year account of Egypt is among the most captivating of experiences. He is a true intellectual in every sense of the word, and at a time of interreligious confusion he lived as a proud Egyptian Copt, unrestrained by institutions of state or church, fearless and forthright, unapologetic about his identity or his love for his country. His friends hail from the far right to the far left of the political spectrum, all holding him in extremely high regard, and those who recall the old days still call him *al-Za'im* (the Leader). Since he remains insistent on not chronicling his own life, I am forced to disclose that at least a glimpse of it lives on in these essays. For his support, insight, guidance, and friendship, I am infinitely grateful.

Many thanks to my brother Essam Farag and his lovely wife Mira Farag, who attended to me during the writing of this manuscript and gave me sufficient fodder for argument and debate.

My late mother Magda El-Badramany, an accomplished psychiatrist who worked overtime until her illness debilitated her, continues to represent in my eyes the quintessential upright, resilient Egyptian woman. She never lived to see this rapture in Egyptian history, but I imagine her reactions to every twist and turn in events, and wonder what she would say.

My life partner, from whom I have learned the meanings of love and honesty, has been my anchor throughout this dizzying journey. This book is as much a product of her work as it is mine. Thank you for tolerating me throughout this upending experience. As has been true for many Egyptians, the revolution's struggle has taken a toll on us all and thrown us off our tracks. Were it not for her reminding me of my bearings, I would have long ago lost my way.

To my friends, colleagues, associates, and confidants, whom I list in no particular order: Khody Akhavi, Timothy Kaldas, John Jirik, Mohamed Sabe, Aniello Alioto, Ehaab Abdou, Nadine Wahab, Shady Taha, Sarah Faragallah, Bilal Qureshi, Maureen Clements, Karim Eskaf,

Wael Ghoneim, Sherif Sobhy Aziz, GemyHood, Sabah Hamamou, Zeinab Abul-Magd, Hafez El-Mirazi, Douglas Boyd, Mohammed el-Nawawy, Ayman Mohyeldin, Hossam Bahgat, Ibrahim El-Hodeiby, Shahira Amin, Sarah El-Sirgany, Omar Shoeb, Sarah Topol, Wael Abbas, Ramy Faragallah, Aliaa Mossalam, Yehia Shawkat, Bassem Youssef, Hicham A. Hellyer, Ibrahim El-Batout, Khaled Abu-l-Naga, Maged Maher Gabra, Paul Sedra, Anthony Shenouda, Vivian Ibrahim, Tamim Al-Barghouti, Mohammed Saeed Ezzeldin, Nancy Okail, Michael Atallah, Mohamed Awwad, Ahmed Gilani, Hala Elshayyal, Ahmed Toughan, the late Khairy Shalaby, the late Mohammed Ouda, Linda Herrera, Bassam Haddad, Hesham Sallam, Malihe Razazan, Kathy Hannah Laughlin, Dena Takruri, Mohammed Shehab Eldin, Nick Oxenhorn, Amro Ali, Dina Shehata, Bassem Hafez, Ahmed Nagy, Ezzat Amin, Jessica Malaty, Hossam El-Hamalawy, Lina Wardani, Fatemah Farag, Sultan Al-Qassemi, Bassam Haddad, Ziad Abu-Rish, Omar Offendum, the Narcycist, Kaila-Lee Clarke, Mayssam Zaroura, Shawn Jackson, and many others. Thank you all.

To the folks at the American University in Cairo Press: thank you, Randi Danforth, for your patience and perseverance, and the terrific Trevor Naylor, Neil Hewison, Nadia Naqib, Laila Ghali, the diligent copyeditor Abdalla Hassan, and project editor Johanna Baboukis.

To the Georgetown University community, which has been my home for the last few years, I am grateful for your kind support and the intellectual haven you have granted me—especially the faculty and staff of the Center for Contemporary Arab Studies (CCAS), including Michael C. Hudson, Samer Shehata, Osama Abi-Mershed, Rochelle Davis, Margaret Daher, Marina Kerkorian, Rania Kiblawi, Zeina Seikaly, and Kelli Harris. At the Communication, Culture, and Technology (CCT) program, my appreciation goes to David Lightfoot, Kimberly Meltzer, Heather Kerst, Sarah Thompson, and Shane Hoon. To my students at Georgetown, who for five semesters, from spring of 2011 until the spring of 2013, tolerated the unpredictability and uncertainty of my courses while Egypt and the region seemed to implode, I am thankful to you for your insight into the developments as they unfolded, which made for thrilling and enlightening conversation, and numerous teaching moments for educators even more so than students.

Elliott Colla and Hesham Salam, my two co-conveners of a weekly seminar series at Georgetown under the banner of the Egyptian Revolution Working Group (ERWG), have served as corrective sounding boards for the ideas and suppositions I have reached along the way. I am fortunate to have benefited from the space they created for scholars on Egypt to deliberate and contest. This experience has been invaluable to me and to this book.

To the friends at *Egypt Independent* now and then, thank you for taking on my writing and encouraging me to contribute, especially the tireless Lina Attalah, the thoughtful Ahmad Shokr, and the inspired Dina K. Hussein. A publication that runs largely on the energy and dynamism of its staff and a committed global readership, *Egypt Independent* has had to break new ground for English-language press in Egypt. This was done on a shoestring budget, despite an often stubborn and undervaluing attitude from the parent company, and during an uncompromisingly difficult time for journalism in the country.

And to the contrarians and agitators I have come to know over the years, of whom there are many, thank you for the adrenaline rushes.

Introduction

I t was midafternoon on Friday, June 18, 2010 in Alexandria and the sun was blazing overhead. Barely a minute had passed since we arrived at the corniche for the silent vigil. I was already extremely uncomfortable, perturbed, and paranoid. The police, across the street so far but keeping a watchful eye, were still within striking distance if given the order. This was unlike other protests in that it was quiet, somber, and non-confrontational. While this was meant to give us strength, we felt extremely vulnerable. We lined up facing the glistening waters of the Mediterranean Sea in a pose that resembled meditation, but our minds were overflowing with ideas and worries. Would we be arrested? Could we be tortured and meet the same fate as Khaled Said, whom we were here to commemorate? It was smart not to confront the police, as we were wildly outnumbered on that day, but it felt extremely evasive not to at least face them. I remember turning back every few moments to make sure I wasn't about to be struck with a baton on the head. Eventually the signal came. The officers had been given notice to disperse the vigil. We were shooed off the premises, and so we began to walk quietly in single file along the beachfront, seeking out new real estate to continue our protest. It was at that moment that I felt an impending worry, perhaps a visceral and existential fear, and decided I could no longer be there. I crossed the street and watched the rest of the procession and the incessant harassment from the police from a safe distance. That day nothing dramatic happened. We felt victorious.

Egypt has been in a state of revolution for years, some say decades, other claim millennia. I believe them all. From the mythical battle between Horus and Sct and Akhenaten's overhaul of theology, art, and statecraft in the thirteenth century BC to the 1919 revolution and the 1952 military coup, the country's oft-cited stability is overly exaggerated. Instead, its history is filled with confrontation, contestation, and transition. Yet despite this, Egypt's seven-thousand-year history had never witnessed anything akin to the popular uprising of 2011, now known as the January 25 Revolution. This makes it worthy of detailed chronicling, careful examination, meditative reflection, and serious interrogation as it etches its place in the history of luminous contemporary revolutions alongside the French, Russian, and American.

The essays in this collection were all written in the three-year period between August 2010 and April 2013, encompassing the final months leading up to the explosion of protests and beyond the first presidential elections, which brought the Muslim Brotherhood's Muhammad Morsi to power at a precarious and turbulent time in the country's history. Many of them grew out of columns written for the English edition of *Al-Masry Al-Youm (Egypt Independent)*, some from other publications such as *Jadaliyya*, and a few have never been published before. The essays delve into the political, economic, social, and cultural climate in Egypt during various junctures in the country's most difficult and unpredictable period.

The book is divided into three sections, each comprising essays pertaining to a specific period and theme. The first section, "The End Days," includes essays written during the six months prior to the eruption of protests in the country on January 25, 2011 and through until the toppling of Mubarak on February 11. These essays address some of the conditions, circumstances, and dynamics characteristic of that period, which made this uprising inevitable. Although it is virtually impossible to exhaustively cover all the preliminary matters ahead of the eruption of protests, these essays are meant to provoke further critique and interrogation, perhaps forcing us to ask more questions than we answer.

It includes essays like "Reclaiming Silence," which chronicles the steady recapturing of the streets by dissenters and the accumulation of confidence and power. While it is a gross mischaracterization to continue referring to the Egyptian revolution as a completely peaceful one, since protesters battled police and thugs for days to hold Tahrir and other major squares in other cities, yet we can begin to see that the philosophical roots of this protest movement commenced with silence. "Geddo and Messianic Football" reflects upon the hypnotic nature of football as a means of distraction from the politics of disempowerment and endemic economic woes. It also lays down the foundations of a deep-seated sense of loyalty and allegiance to both club and nation that birthed the football Ultras fans, now the vanguard in Egyptian revolutionary action, and groups that have waged war against the security forces during the eighteen days of protest and beyond, including most recently the so-called Black Bloc. "On Marina and Chávez" speaks to the social ills of economic disparity and the elite bubble. Of course the revolution itself has helped burst that bubble in significant ways, but the burden of responsibility for society's most needy remains an utmost priority. The essay barely scratches the surface of a colossal labor movement that brought the state to its knees ahead of the revolutionary action and continues to be the only guarantee of fundamental change in the country.

"The Simulacra of Religious Intolerance" was written to document the intransigent dogma of exploited religion and speaks to a need for secular criticism in the Saidian tradition as a source of political critique to avoid the intractable sanctimonious protection of political discourse. With the rise of the Salafi movements as contenders on the Egyptian scene, securing 25 percent of the first elected parliament after the revolution, and their significant financial and ideological reach, a novel challenge to identity and politics will likely emerge in the months and years to come as the erratic nature of the revolutionary intelligentsia butts heads with the tiered hierarchy of most Egyptian Islamist organizations. A piece once written for a specific moment, it has nevertheless taken on a new meaning in light of the shifting discourse on religion and politics in the country.

"Learning to Mourn with the Poles" should be read as a call to rehistoricize at a time when illusion triumphs over experience. Dealing with national tragedy, the essay addresses the burdens of national mistakes, pleading that we take responsibility for the ills of both state and government: the Egyptian public acknowledging its failure to take back government from those who abused it; discovering the falsification of public life; understanding that while 1952 is still known as a revolution, the nomenclature should now change to describe it more accurately as a coup d'état that brought the military to power for sixty years.

On the topic of growing regional and global influence, "Never Say No to the Panda" discusses the asymmetry of power in geostrategic ways and Egypt's declining economic sovereignty. With the country being pulled in opposite directions by its desperate need for funds and resources, it is likely to succumb to the will of external powers—on one end by the United States, the International Monetary Fund, and the European Union, and on the other by Saudi Arabia, Qatar, and other Gulf countries. Each has placed conditions unappealing to the nation's rulers or the public at large, further damaging public life. But neither of these two poles attempts to solve the crisis that brought revolution to Egypt—neoliberal policies of aggressive privatization and strengthened entrepreneurship at the expense of the masses. Egypt may have to learn from the Chinese what a complex system not beholden and enslaved to the global economy might look like. Yet this will likely come at a hefty cost to Egypt by rendering it more dependent.

The elections of November 2010, arguably the most farcical process to date in Egypt, are the subject of "Best in Show." They are also a precursor to what is now a circus of electoral theater of the absurd, as the parliamentary elections brought candidates from parties that never existed and less than 5 percent of Egyptian voters knew the people they were told to vote for before going to the polls. With the state supervising at least eight electoral processes (constitutional referendum, three rounds of parliamentary elections for the lower house, two for the upper house, and two rounds of presidential elections) in two years, Egypt has become a "republic of elections." With each stage, the state perfects the mechanism of processing public opinion while still controlling the gauges. From the farcical disqualification processes of the presidential contenders to the irrefutability and absolute immunity of the Presidential Election Commission, these are the former ruling National Democratic Party's parliamentary elections but with new players on the field. "The Hegemony of Sharks" continues this line of thought but suggests the power of misdirection, distraction, and monopolization of the social construction of reality.

Other essays, like "The End of Illegitimacy," speak of the social ills of Egyptian society and the wrath of taboo and stigma that obliterate both the state's and the public's sense of responsibility for their outliers. By defining its fringes, rather than attempting to incorporate them, it shuns them. Emphasis on remedy through denial or punishment does not resolve the problem as much as it allows it to fester in a subterranean manner. Today hundreds of thousands of young Egyptians in every major city, especially Cairo, are growing up in the streets and slums with little familial support or safety, all largely because the state and the public have decided national honor and pride are more important to preserve than their livelihood. Egypt has no honor unless it can safeguard its weakest members. All of Egypt's children are legitimate.

This section also includes essays that discuss the explosion of dissident action, including the final triggers that led to the moment when all the configurations and calculations did not add up, yet something extraordinary happened. With that logic, the defiance and will of protesters remains the only true safeguard for the continuation of the revolution. "Coptic Exodus from Disneyland" discusses the awakening of Egypt's Christians in the aftermath of the 2011 New Year's Eve bombing of the Two Saints Church in Alexandria to the fact that the state had abandoned them. The essay attempts to see populist power in Egypt as successful only if Christian invisibility, compliance, disengagement, and fear dissipate. Arguably, it is as early as the Umraniya incident in Giza, just a month before the revolution erupted, when Coptic youth confronted the police, that the so-called 'protected minority' turned on its guardian. It was also the first time in recent memory that Christians fought with the security forces, and was the first explosion of violent dissent against the state ahead of January 25.

"Ablaze the Body Politic" charts the power of the intangible idea of inspiration, how Tunisia nourished Egypt, and how the *corpus politicus* ("body politic") became the true anatomy and physiology of the public. This is the precursor to the masses congealing into collectives, suffering simultaneously in both the singular and the plural. What comes to one comes to many. The last two essays of this section, "The Gravity of Pharaohs" and "Dared to Defy," bookmark the revolution's success. The former deals with the recognition of an impending finitude to the regime of Hosni Mubarak and the shattering of the fear barrier. It is the ability to identify when absolute power all of a sudden looks frail and when authoritarianism turns on its head, when the strong shrinks and the weak becomes omnipotent. It is the naive epiphany that the end is near. The latter commemorates the fact that all odds were stacked against Egypt's revolutionaries at the outset and their defiance is at least a moment to behold. This essay was not written with the intention of celebrating preemptively or with the supposition that the revolution had effectively succeeded, but rather stopped to commemorate the unlikeliness of what had just taken place.

The second section, "Revolution Interrupted?," looks at the hurdles placed before the revolution to derail its forward motion. From a labyrinthine maze in "On Constitutional Reform" and clunky state journalism in "Liberating the Media" to the rise of *baltagiya* (thugs) in "The Ax-bearers" as a legal and social category and a tool used, both literally and rhetorically, to manipulate the political scene, this section deals with the revolution veering off course. Other essays focus on paternalism in Egypt.

This includes the role of the military in "Revolutionary Fatigues," which chronicles the top brass's exhaustion of the revolutionaries and dressing the uprising in military attire. The next essay, "Who's Your Daddy?," tackles the continuing battle against the patriarchs of society.

"After Maspero" narrates the story of Egypt's social fabric following the tragic massacre of Coptic protesters on October 9, 2011, including the military's miscalculation and the rise of another revolutionary icon, Mina Danial, from the carnage of this crisis. In the context of minority rights, "Of Men and Hymen" challenges the discussion surrounding gender, empowerment, and representation in Egypt. By disentangling systematic misogyny, the essay examines the overlapping spaces of sexuality and revolution.

"The Lost Tribe" discusses the diaspora, their longtime estrangement from Egyptian politics, their disenchantment with the electoral process, and their faith in the revolution outside of politics. Another essay, "The Three-Horned Bull," describes how all the presidential scenarios ahead of the 2012 elections were favorable for the ruling military irrespective of the choices and how hegemony delivers at the polls. In almost every circumstance, the country is heading in the direction of confrontation, uncertainty, and general dismay for the masses as their revolution becomes the subject of high-level battles and backroom dealings.

The final section, "Ad Infinitum," argues that the revolution will never end, because it is rooted in both people's memories and the creation of modern Egyptian myths as well as collective experiences of both resisting the regime and rejoicing in its downfall. The essays here trace the evidence that the revolution is not only alive and well but will remain part of Egypt's new political reality for years to come. It is the gauge of national success and the barometer of governmental prospects. "The Conscientious Objectors" discusses the boycott campaign that preceded the presidential election and the gradual disinterest in elections and their processes. Egypt's new politics actually reside outside the ballot boxes, yet the use of fear and panic were paramount to drive participation up in the first presidential election in the post-Mubarak era.

With a newly elected president, "Morsi's Debts" raises the questions of affiliation, allegiance, and loyalty for the Brotherhood candidate whose connections to the Islamist group run perhaps too deep for him to be pragmatic in a multipolar Egypt. "Year of the Ostrich" describes the military's public image and its ability to manage its perception during the transition period, and how that may bode well for its longevity, publicly and backstage. "A Seven A" discusses the newfound importance of profanity in freedom of expression before and since the revolution.

With religion playing an increasingly visible role in Egyptian politics, especially with a new Islamist constitution serving as the country's new legal blueprint, questions about the role that al-Azhar and the Coptic Church will play in the coming era raise both concern and ire. The essay "Patron Saints" presents ways in which struggles for control of the highest seat of Islamic research and religious jurisprudence complicate the actions of the institution and introduce unaffiliated dogmatic groups.

More articles identify the relationship between events and news in Egypt today. "Tragedy and Farce" discusses the level of media professionalism so as to contort incidents and events to serve as a corrective to news. "The State of Anarchy" is a momentary intervention into the discussion about anarchy in the revolution. I argue here that anarchism did not commence when it became convenient for the revolutionary activists, as it is often described. Rather I make the case that Egypt itself is anarcho-syndicalist and has become increasingly so since the revolution. And while the landscape of the country's 'political theater' remained largely opaque, "New Face" discusses the unrecognizability of major players and the rapid transformation of rhetoric in the period after Morsi's ascent. How does one read political decisions and actions? Can we take political posturing and positioning at face value?

"Media Forms" revisits the changing media spaces and how they help to both undermine and reinforce the revolutionary impulse in an unstable Egypt. The last three essays are "Lemons and Raisins" on revolutionaries and Islamists, "Blood Ballots" on the legitimacy of electioneering in conjunction with repeated instability and bloodshed on the streets, and "A Nation Derailed" on the government's malaise in responding to consecutive railway tragedies as a metaphor of institutional incompetence.

The first elected president, Muhammad Morsi, brings to the office many unpaid burdens. He must balance many conflicting interests and may be destined to fail irrespective of his actions. Whom does he owe and how can he move forward? Nothing less than the independence of the presidency, the judiciary, and the legislative branches are at stake in a long-term tug-of-war between the various powers in the Egyptian polity—the military, the Muslim Brotherhood, and the courts. The existence and growing strength of a third political tier is necessary and imperative but hinges on the ability to assert independence from the military. While

Morsi may not pay his debts to the revolution, can the judiciary find its independence from the executive, legislative, and military powers?

While these essays focus telescopically on the two-year period of the revolution, it is important to note that the seeds of the revolution were sown in a decades-long struggle by Egypt's workers, farmers, syndicates, poets, journalists, lawyers, and literati, which is discussed more extensively and comprehensively in other works. As for these modest musings and meditations about Egypt at a crossroads, they are meant to highlight the fault lines that render these two years extraordinary with all of their contradictions, complications, peaks, and troughs.

On June 18, 2010 in Alexandria, as we stood silent, we felt victorious when nothing dramatic happened to us at the hands of the police. Since then, everything dramatic has indeed happened. And yet we do not feel victorious. It must mean we are still in flux.

I

THE END DAYS

Anyone who has the power to make you believe absurdities
has the power to make you commit injustices.

— Voltaire

The two citizens who tried to set themselves ablaze in front of the building of the People's Assembly last week were driven by personal reasons.
It is wrong to cite just two examples of self-immolation and say this is a
common phenomenon. Their motives were personal. It is quite wrong to
allege that they were making political demands.

— Fathi Surur, speaker of parliament, January 19, 2011

Until they become conscious they will never rebel, and until after they
have rebelled they cannot become conscious.

— George Orwell, *1984*

We are hungry! Eighteen days have already elapsed this month!

— Chant of striking workers, Dayr al-Medina, Egypt, circa 1170 BCE

If I could meet the Sultan, I would say to him:
O, Sultan
Your hounds tore my clothes
Your agents are always behind me
Their eyes are behind me
Their noses are behind me
Their feet are behind me
Like certain fate, like eternal justice
They question my wife
And write
The names of my friends
O, ye children
You are the spring rain . . . the wheat spikes of hope
You are the fertile seeds of our sterile lives
You are the generation that will defeat defeat.

— Nizar Qabbani, *Margin Notes on the Book of Defeat* (1967)

Reclaiming Silence

July 22, 2010

E gypt has never been known for its quietness. The throngs of tourists that visit its capital every year observe the bustling commotion of the metropolis, the loudness of the streets, and the high decibel level of spoken Egyptian. Sporting celebrations and traditional weddings often erupt in ear-piercing festivities. Attempts at controlling gratuitous use of the car horn often fall on deaf ears. An exodus of Cairo's affluent out of the busy hubs to new suburban residential developments is often rationalized on the grounds of seeking tranquillity.

What is normal in Egypt likely qualifies as noise pollution in other parts of the world. And the threshold for noise in Egypt would warrant the issuance of violation notices in many countries. This extends to human interaction. Egyptians are loud, expressive, and boisterous conversationalists. Silence rarely plays a role in their daily affairs. In some countries, like Japan and Finland, silence is a fundamental component of basic social interaction and often denotes respect and friendliness. Many religious traditions, from Buddhism and Hinduism to Sufism and Trappist Catholicism, implore adherents to observe total silence, in order to raise worship to meditative levels and express complete devotion and supplication. Among the Native American Western Apaches of the United States, silence is a specific strategy deployed in observation and anticipation of the other person's expression and behavior, before taking action or articulating a response. It is most commonly used during times of uncertainty or anger, precisely the conditions when the average Egyptian is inclined to vocalize.

Therefore it comes with some degree of irony that the word of greatest salience in Egypt this week is in fact 'silence.' Since the brutal beating and death of the now-iconic Alexandrian young man Khaled Said, a Facebook group with 200,000 members has publicized one silent protest after the next to protest police brutality, demand justice for Said, and call for an end to the Emergency Law. The latest installment of these quiet protestations, where participants are asked to dress in black and stand side by side along the waterfronts of Cairo and Alexandria while reading their Qur'ans or Bibles, falls on the fifty-eighth anniversary of the 1952 coup. The group members have named this the "Silent Revolution" and hope to exceed the numbers gathered in previous protests.

But silence is not new to Egyptians. Political scientists and learned observers often produce accounts of political suppression during various periods in Egypt's contemporary history, showing that the muzzling of dissent has become part and parcel of the fabric of Egyptian expression. Yet, despite the often clichéd image of the apathetic, laissez-faire attitude Egyptians are said to have vis-à-vis politics, silence as strength rather than subservience has a surprisingly long history in Egypt.

More than 4,500 years ago, the ancient Egyptian vizier Ptahhotep of the Fifth Dynasty wrote a manual of instructions that taught his successors how to perfect the craft of fine speech with rules derived from religious principles and practical psychology. The first canon of Egyptian rhetoric was silence. It was described as a moral posture and tactic, not to be confused with passivity or quietism. Ptahhotep wrote that when arguing with a superior, "bow your back and be silent; he will confound himself and be thought a fool."

Silence is thus a response. Another 3,100-year-old manual of instructions by the Nineteenth Dynasty scribe Amenemope expresses admiration for Maat (The Truly Silent Man) or "one who succeeds by virtue of his unflagging inner repose and self-control." A Truly Silent Man is he who is characterized by humility, quiet demeanor, generosity, honesty, and piety. These personal qualities are both derived from and named after the goddess Maat. She wore a feather atop her head, which she weighed against the souls of the deceased to determine their eligibility for the afterlife, a gesture that reflected the virtues of truth, justice, and order. Over three thousand years later, an extremely successful cyber-campaign for Khaled Said hopes to mobilize tens of thousands of its "truly silent" members this Friday to demand that the virtues of Maat be upheld.

However, naysayers, skeptics, and critics of technological determinism will argue that the majority of Egyptians will steer clear of the "silent revolution," as they have in similar protests over the last few decades. They will argue that fear, paranoia, and limited access to the Internet will ensure the Khaled Said typhoon is no more than a tempest in a teacup. They will have enough evidence to warrant such an argument. Until recently, political life in Egypt has been an exemplary case of what political and mass communication theorists describe as "the spiral of silence." Thirty-six years ago, the German political scientist Elizabeth Noelle-Neumann used this term to refer to the disappearance of minority voices. She postulated that to avoid isolation, people who hold fringe or dissenting views will either alter their ideas to conform to the majority's position or resort to silence, thus furthering the impression that the majority's view is dominant.

This theory has often been criticized on the grounds that when individual or group support are present and where interpersonal relationships have a greater impact on one's views than impersonal public opinion, the spiral of silence dissipates. With the social-networking portal Facebook serving as the ultimate liaison between the interpersonal and the public as well as creating solidarity, dissent, and community in a comparatively safe environment, the online spiral of silence appears to have been overcome. Those who once feared having their names associated with any form of opposition, irrespective of its subtlety, increasingly participate in the public campaign for Khaled Said without concern for retribution. And for those who believe Facebook is still the dominion of the wealthy, they must contend with the latest news of the social networking behemoth crossing the landmark of half a billion users, more than a tenth of the world's population.

Nevertheless, the success of the silent protest will depend largely on whether the outrage surrounding Said and other cases of police brutality can break the spiral of silence. It has often puzzled political theorists and observers why some societal conditions are able to subdue expression and create silence in the face of injustice. Those who witnessed atrocities in Nazi Germany, apartheid South Africa, Palestine, and elsewhere and said nothing may have fallen victim to the spiral of silence. South African Nobel Prize laureates in literature J.M. Coetzee and Nadine Gordimer paint powerful images of characters whose silence furthered and prolonged apartheid, yet in other instances was an act of resistance.

At the end of the day, silence has rarely been a crime in itself. In fact, the right to observe silence is an accepted legal protection enjoyed by people undergoing police interrogation or trial in many countries. Ironically, what Egypt's Facebook youth for Khaled Said may inadvertently be demanding with their "silent revolution" is the inalienable right to be protected in their silence, a virtue their ancestors taught the world millennia ago.

July 23 marked the fifty-eighth anniversary of the end of the monarchy and the birth of the Egyptian republic. All three Egyptian presidents since 1952—Gamal Abd al-Nasser, Anwar al-Sadat, and Hosni Mubarak—have used heavy-handed approaches to maintain a firm grip on power while allowing for occasional political expression to air out the pressure pot of anger and frustration in Egyptian society. This summer, possibly a landmark period in modern Egyptian politics, it appears the regime has little control over political dissent in the country.

Many observers believe the current maelstrom in Egypt is a perfect storm, with some western media overzealously and prematurely declaring this the end of an era. Yet virtually every article about the impending post-Mubarak era declares that Egypt is a nation filled with reluctant dissent and political passivity, including references to the pharaonic roots of Egyptian subservience to authority. Yet there is significant evidence to the contrary.

While presidential hopeful Mohamed ElBaradei seems to monopolize coverage of the opposition movement, beneath the headlines, Egypt's youth are abuzz and it has little to do with ElBaradei. Initially an online sensation, the ElBaradei campaign has already made the transition from alternative to traditional media. This may be a coming of age for his campaign, but it left an online framework for dissent, giving us a glimpse of the Internet's growing potential in Egypt.

This potential was tested on June 7, when a twenty-eight-year-old Alexandrian, Khaled Said, was brutalized by policemen at an Internet café. With a large number of people witnessing the event, few believed the state's assertion that Said died due to asphyxiation from swallowing a bag of drugs. At best it seemed like a clumsy mistake and at worst an intentional cover-up by the police. The following day a Facebook group called "We Are All Khaled Said" was created to protest the incident. A leaked image of Khaled's contorted, bloody face went viral. In just five weeks, the Facebook group boasted 200,000 members, a feat for Egyptian social networking groups.

Unlike any other fan page, "We Are All Khaled Said" is a bustling metropolis of public expression and activism. In a short month, the group's members have staged three major silent protests against police brutality across Egypt, many of which were replicated by Egyptians living abroad, including London,

Washington, D.C., Abu Dhabi, and Sydney. The most prominent characteristic of all these expressions of dissent is the uncanny silence.

Described by some as flash mobs, these protests have called on Egyptians young and old, men and women, parents and children to wear black during one of the country's hottest summer seasons and converge on the waterfronts of the Nile and sea from Alexandria to Aswan. They are asked to stand, side by side, in silent contemplation and read from Qur'ans and Bibles.

Stand they did. With each protest, the numbers swelled, documentation with cameras and phones became more adept, and the mobilization was more effective. Conversely, the state has responded with a substantial show of force, in some cases deploying thousands of police for every handful of silent protesters. The results are Tiananmen Square–like photographs juxtaposing the peaceful protesters and the state's police authority, which only further enraged the public and provoked more protests.

The Facebook page called for a rapturous-yet-inaudible crescendo last Friday, July 23, the anniversary of the "Free Officers" coup. The Facebook youth ambitiously declared it the "silent revolution" and used popular cultural depictions of anti-authoritarian motifs, such as a subtitled montage of speeches from the Wachowski brothers' film *V for Vendetta*, to popularize the protest.

The group's unique mobilization and decentralization methods have led to surprisingly high participation. The average posting on the page receives over two hundred comments, and the group's regular opinion surveys on how to strategize are often completed by thousands of participants within hours after posting. All decisions in the group are determined by polls, from calls to inscribe banknotes with messages like "No to the Emergency Law. No to torture. This is our country. We are all Khaled Said" to a Facebook message campaign directed at police officers' profiles, imploring them to refrain from torture. It appears the group's strength comes not only from its egalitarian disposition but also, dare I say, democratic procedure, an exception in statist Egypt today.

This equal participation on the Facebook page has mobilized tens of thousands of youth to identify with a diffuse yet unrelenting social justice movement and translate cyber-solidarity into street protests.

The groups' continued success so far comes from the organizers' ability to protect their anonymity, and more importantly, from safeguarding their anti-torture message from both state pressure and political opportunism.

Rather than seek hyperbolic goals like regime change, the group has three clear objectives—absolute justice for Khaled Said, an end to torture and police brutality in all its forms, and an end to the Emergency Law. This focus and clarity in mission and the message's appeal to all Egyptians has effectively immunized the Khaled Said movement from mediocrity, modest expectations, and state criticism.

While change is in the air, its sluggishness may be dampening hopes again. Nevertheless, for the Facebook youth—the thousands who all go by the moniker Khaled Said—their successive bouts of silence, despite their colossal disadvantage, amount to rare thunderclaps over the Nile.

Geddo and Messianic Football

August 5, 2010

A big story has monopolized the Egyptian press for days. Not the likelihood of war between Israel and Lebanon, not the country's forthcoming water crisis and negotiations in Uganda with the Nile Basin nations, not the debate surrounding presidential succession, not the price of meat ahead of the fasting month of Ramadan, and not the Israeli siege of Gaza next door. Instead, the topic of conversation is Muhammad Nagi Ismail, the Egyptian football star commonly known as Geddo. The topic of his complicated and costly transfer from his Alexandrine club Ittihad (United) to one of the two Cairo giants, al-Ahly or Zamalek, has been a subject of contention between the two clubs, their supporters, and anyone with an interest in Egyptian football (which seems like the majority of the population).

Geddo burst onto the scene in epic fashion during the Africa Cup of Nations this year and immediately preceding the World Cup, which saw Egypt eliminated in an explosive marathon of matches against Algeria. For a country angered and humiliated by its inability to qualify for the top competition, and in a show of what some commentators described as "divine justice," Geddo came on as substitute for the Egyptian team and scored within minutes of play in five consecutive matches. His scoring average of one goal for every thirty-five minutes puzzled sports statisticians and delighted Egyptians. When Egypt was crowned African Champion in January, Geddo was the tournament's top scorer and the country's savior par excellence.

But what did Geddo save Egypt from? He had not fed the hungry, sheltered the homeless, treated the ailing, solved water shortage problems, improved the quality of education, conquered corruption, taken on rampant sexual harassment, curbed domestic violence, burst the real estate bubble, or anything of the sort. Instead, he saved Egypt from Egypt. A nation increasingly aware of its receding role in regional politics, Egyptians are now sensitive to national blunders and pained by the all-too-frequent injuries to collective pride. It comes as no secret that almost every development indicator in Egypt is in decline, with the exception of literacy rates and access to communication. The executive summary of the 2010 Egypt Human Development Report states that "the most striking and unusual finding" of the report is the "extent to which youth are excluded from political and civic participation." Why this would strike anyone as a surprise is beyond my comprehension.

Egypt has been actively depoliticizing its populace since at least the mid-1970s. Despite the hoopla about energizing the youth base of the ruling National Democratic Party (NDP) and the eruption of online activism through social networking sites, the majority of Egyptian youth are politically unengaged. Conveniently but not coincidentally, political ineptness and aloofness have an inversely proportional relationship to football fandom. This is the subject of a delightfully incisive book entitled *Masr bitil'ab* (Egypt is Playing) on the transformation of the Egyptian people from a *sha'b* (people) to a *jumhur* (audience). Authored by Muhammad Tawfiq and published recently by Dar al-Masri, the book historicizes this trend dating back to the days of the first Egyptian team, al-Ahly, in 1909.

Tawfiq asserts that "participation" in Egyptian football events now comes at a time when the country no longer leads the region in science, art, literature, music, politics, technology, agriculture, or any other field of knowledge, practical or esoteric. However, he gives a plausible explanation for why football has so easily displaced politics in the lives of Egyptians. Fundamentally, the sport is the polar opposite of politics. Football is the only justifiable and legally permissible reason for tens, if not hundreds, of thousands to congregate, either in celebration or in public mourning. It is the only institution in the country where talent, performance, and execution are measures of success—the ultimate meritocracy that defies the omnipresent *wasta* (connections). Despite the Abougreishas and the Imams (two prominent Egyptian footballing families), football is the only dominion exempt from hereditary succession. It is the only competition where results alone determine success, where retirement comes when productivity falls, and where a good work ethic is the only way to get ahead. And shockingly, it is the one realm where the security apparatus is there to protect these rules rather than rewrite them.

While all these characteristics suffice to explain why football is more than just the 'beautiful game' to Egyptians, the icing on the cake is the fact that people are the true judges of quality and outcome. In a completely transparent field where the smallest detail in the operation is subject to the scrutiny of every member of our public-turned-audience, we are all coaches, jurors, experts, authorities, and elites. In a nation where social inequalities are rapidly growing, football IQ (not political wherewithal) is the last test of acuity, where the son of a carpenter can compete with the son of a minister. It is also the most likely profession in which that carpenter's son can climb the socioeconomic ladder to become at least a millionaire, and at best a Geddo.

Before Geddo there was Zizou, preceded by Abu Treka, Hosni, Hadari, Gomaa, Mido, and so on. Players from very humble roots are sought out by the political intelligentsia to gain legitimacy among, and the affection of, the Egyptian public. And legitimacy they garnered, albeit briefly. At no point in the last few years has so much public support been expressed for the highest echelons of the NDP as shortly after the final World Cup qualifying fiasco between Egypt and Algeria in Omdurman, Sudan. It was a time when "benign nationalism," as Tamim Al-Barghouti calls it, reared its ugly head. The national and private media marched to the jingoistic tune of a Pied Piper proclaiming that Egyptian dignity had taken a blow and had to be defended.

Television commentators like Amr Adib, Khalid al-Ghandur, and company took the airwaves by storm, treating the match and claims of attacks by Algerian fans in Sudan after the whistle as if it were Egypt's 9/11. Flag lapel pins appeared, nationalistic music roared from televisions and radios alike, and the Egyptian blogosphere and Facebook were alight with commotion. Football, or what some call the "opium of the masses," had combined with propaganda and incitement to produce a chorus of antagonism that easily qualifies as hate media beaming with chauvinism, ethnocentrism, and xenophobia. In one instance, a television host suggested that Egyptians should take to the streets to kill Algerians and exact justice for the so-called crimes committed against their brethren in Sudan. The manner in which consent was manufactured and fanaticism fostered meets the conditions of what the world-renowned linguist Noam Chomsky calls "propaganda models."

By international broadcasting standards and laws governing media content, this expression was not unlike similar calls by hate radio station

RTLM in Rwanda that implored and mobilized Hutus to slaughter Tutsis, precipitating genocide. By international norms, Egyptian satellite broadcasters who exploited the public's sentiments to orchestrate a crescendo of anti-Algerian frenzy should be investigated and tried for malpractice, hate speech, and incitement of violence.

The gaping wound of not making it to the 2010 World Cup in South Africa brought the small tranquilizing effect football success had on Egyptians to an abrupt end. The weapon of mass distraction had dissipated and the shroud of glory representing the country's success drifted away. All that remained was a bitter amalgam of dismay and fanaticism. These are the markings of a sad nation, one that needs to be distracted not only from its public failures but also from its football losses. Muhammad Sabe, the editor in chief of popular Egyptian sports portal Filgoal.com, told me that this trend of distraction has been a characteristic of every major football loss. "When the national team was eliminated from the Confederation Cup, the case of players hiring prostitutes was raised, and after the loss to Algeria in Sudan, the incidents of violence were exaggerated."

Lest Egyptians begin to ask pressing questions about their country during the brief hiatus from football in the weeks following the elimination by Algeria, the next tournament presented an opportunity to redeem and comfort a confused and wounded nation. The Africa Cup of Nations provided a chance to have collective dignity reasserted, pride restored, and tranquillity brought back to 83 million audience members. And on January 12, 2010, with most Egyptians bracing for a tough match against World Cup–bound Nigeria, a new messiah was born to return waters back to their streams. Audiences would chant his name, saying, "If you want to demolish him, bring him Geddo." The twenty-five-year-old player from Damanhur mesmerized fans, prophetically resurrected national self-esteem, hypnotized audiences, concealed social ills, postponed introspection, and in the process, "saved" Egypt from Egypt.

On Marina and Chávez

August 19, 2010

I have not seen disparity between the rich and poor as much as I did in the South American cities of São Paolo, Brazil and Caracas, Venezuela. In the Venezuelan capital, rich communities have, over decades, effectively extricated themselves from society and now live on protected property away from regular interaction with the impoverished majority.

With wealth pooled so tightly in the hands of a slim minority—who acquired their fortunes in a wave of aggressive neoliberalization of all industries, starting in the 1970s and continuing until the late 1990s—the majority's socioeconomic conditions have deteriorated under a two-pronged failure of an underfunded, weakened, and bloated government bureaucracy and the inability and disinterest of the private sector to absorb or train an undereducated, unskilled, undermotivated, and desperate majority.

This socioeconomic rift in the Bolivarian republic was precipitated by a growing isolation of the wealthy, who became less inclined to hire from the ranks of the poor, contributed less to charities, and overwhelmingly subscribed to the capitalist logic of "effort begets wealth," evidenced by a few tokenistic examples of rags-to-riches stories from the time of aggressive privatization. Gated communities, surrounded by impenetrable walls, armed security, barbed wire, and watchtowers, rose to house the rich in the Venezuelan cities of Caracas, Valencia, and Maracaibo. The compounds, created to "protect their way of life," were akin to the expatriate refuge compounds in Saudi Arabia, where a cultural enclave can be sustained outside the purview or judgment or desire of the conservative public.

Instead, the Venezuelan elite created their worst nightmare. The self-fulfilling prophecy of a jealous middle and lower class materialized as crime ran rampant in the cities. The upscale Bantustans of the rich precipitated ghettos at their seams. The wake-up call came when elections brought socialist leader Hugo Chávez to power, a man who rode the discontentment of the hungry masses by vowing to reverse policies that protect the rich, to nationalize the oil industry, and to redistribute the country's wealth.

The lifestyle of Egypt's wealthy today mirrors that of the Venezuelan elite before the rise of Chávez, with one minor difference—concern. On a recent visit to the country's beautiful islands and affluent Caribbean playground of Moroccoy (a place not unlike Marina in Egypt) on a friend's speedboat, I was privy to many conversations about the country's political situation. While many of the rich remain rich, in the past they had nothing to complain about because the poor majority was comfortably invisible. Today, Chávez's fiery rhetoric of socialism and tightening grip on the elite has made their lavish beach excursions far less carefree.

Today Egypt is looking more like Venezuela of the early 1990s. The latest statistics show that 22 percent of Egyptians are unemployed; that means that more than one in five Egyptians are jobless. Prior to Ramadan, the price of wheat was increased by 20 percent and the cost of meat by 35 percent in what Mohamed El-Barghouthi described as a system of government sabotage against wheat producers in favor of the importers.

Not unlike Venezuela, summers in Egypt are often accented by the mass migration of Cairenes to coastal vacation spots on the beaches of the Mediterranean Sea, known commonly as *al-sahil* (the coast). Eleven years ago, housing expert Milad Hanna described *al-sahil* as an exquisite shoreline, "[a] 'delicious fillet steak' [which] has been devoted to a certain class of people and some professional syndicates, leaving no space for public beaches, turning the coastline into a copy of the Great Wall."

To this day, *al-sahil*'s 'Great Wall' still stands. The massive development of infrastructure and services on the North Coast are often thought to be a sign of upward mobility, since the number of units across one hundred villages and resorts can accommodate several million beach revelers (certainly more than the percentage of wealthy in the country). However, this is not necessarily the case, because the exponential growth of the coast has not meant that a larger proportion of the population now owns property between Alexandria and Marsa Matruh. Rather, it is the same 5 percent of the population that now owns multiple chalets, villas, and palaces, most of which were acquired as real estate investments in a market that continues to appreciate; the growing options only exist to ensure exclusivity.

It is not unusual for members of the Egyptian upper crust to own villas in Marina, Hacienda, and perhaps one of the older, less trendy spots like Aida, Marakia, and Marabella, or a smaller and more secluded (and hence less eventful) resort. These properties are juggled by the economic elite every season depending on their needs—privacy versus commotion, exclusivity versus accessibility, opulence versus modesty, and activity versus tranquillity. These shifting needs will affect the decision to buy, sell, rent, or let the properties ripen. All this is governed by the one rule of "cost is demand."

Nowhere is this more obvious than the new EMAAR project Marassi (formerly Sidi Abd al-Rahman), an ultra-exclusive resort destined to be the next Marina. The grounds, which resemble one of the new university campuses in the Gulf, house two dance clubs that are more exclusive than those frequented by Jay-Z and P. Diddy in the Big Apple. The clientele at these clubs are dressed to perform a pathetic caricature impersonation of western discotheques. Attempting to mimic dancers from Beyoncé, Usher, and Rihanna music videos, the Egyptian elite, who dish out no less than LE 75 ($12) for a shot of whiskey, would barely survive a mere stroll down any Cairo road. But then again, they need not worry about Cairo roads while enveloped by the 'Great Wall.'

The weekend before Ramadan I found myself in a similar circumstance as in Moroccoy, aboard a heftily priced boat in a bay, this time in Marina. As the speedboat wound its way through the artificial canals in Marina's circuitous lakes, I could not get my mind off the plight of the poor. The retail price of the boat I was on was likely no less than LE 500,000 ($80,000). The fuel used to fill its tank could feed a poor family for a month, and it would take the average Egyptian's full salary for eleven years to generate the cost of the boat. Not surprisingly, these contradictions never came up in the friendly exchanges on the boat. No one wanted to disturb the serenity of this bubble. One was to accept that we are evidence of a meritocratic Egypt, at least until my partner responded to the question of what she thought of the country after six months abroad by saying, "Egypt is in trouble." She had disrupted the bliss of amnesia.

A good friend and scholar at the London School of Economics, who visits his home in Egypt every holiday season, expressed the contradictions any empathetic and socially conscious member of the elite faces in his or her daily life. Trapped between the intractable guilt when facing the poor and the repulsively arrogant expressions of status among the consumption-obsessed wealthy, he said, "I cannot tolerate looking at either poverty or wealth in this country."

What this colleague is pointing to is an inevitable byproduct of an increasingly kleptocratic environment. Given the exceptionally high level of corruption, collusion, and embezzlement in Egypt, much of the extravagant wealth in the country today raises unanswered questions. But the pressing questions are the most personal. When will the Egyptian upper class begin questioning their lifestyle? When will unhappiness, overload, anxiety, non-fulfillment, and guilt at a blindingly militant pursuit of more material goods come to an end? When will the unsustainable obsession with accumulating wealth and possessions falter? When will the rich in Egypt exhibit symptoms of affluenza?

Regardless of how high the walls they erect to hide from the realities of a failing state are, or how often they bounce from one coastal cocoon to the next to avoid the 'undesirable' masses, or how few conversations they have about hunger and the price of wheat, Egypt's wealthy are destined for a wake-up call.

The Simulacra of Religious Intolerance

September 16, 2010

Tolerance is a very peculiar thing. Not only is it both a sentiment and a behavior, it is also characterized by its antagonist. To be tolerant, one must not only learn to accept the existence of one's opposition, adversary, and counterpoint, but also learn that the intolerance of others poses the greatest threat. Should a tolerant person tolerate the intolerance of others?

In history, most intolerance is eventually met with intolerance. Girolamo Savonarola, a radical Dominican cleric and ruler of Florence for four years in the late fifteenth century, had declared war on the Renaissance and all its symbols. He had imposed a zero tolerance policy toward all knowledge creation outside of his conception of the world. Everything from Sandro Botticelli's paintings to ancient poetry, along with his detractors, were set alight in a public ceremonial burning known as "Bonfire of the Vanities." The religious institutions of the time, namely the papal seat under Alexander VI, did not follow in the teachings of its Lord Jesus Christ who once preached, "Love your enemies, bless them that curse you, do good to them that hate you." Rather, Alexander VI ordered Savonarola's excommunication and execution on charges of heresy. The radical cleric faced the same fate as the subjects of his fiery rampages. He was burned at the site of his bonfires in Florence's Piazza della Signoria, where he had destroyed his adversaries and their intellectual output.

So can principled tolerance as a value withstand the temptation of its antonym? Egyptian minister of culture Farouk Hosny is said to have lost his bid as UNESCO head largely because of an "intolerant" quote from May 2008 stating he would himself burn any Israeli book he finds in Egyptian libraries. This comment was deemed inappropriate because it went further than imposing an intellectual boycott on a state that exercises unspeakable horrors against the native Palestinians. Hence the line here is very thin. The American legal system demarcates this distinction at the point where expression becomes criminal action. In the time of Savonarola (with the Gutenberg movable-type press coming into existence just a few decades earlier), manuscripts were all originals that had to be copied by scribes and drafted over extended periods of time. Hence the destruction of knowledge—in the sciences, arts, or letters—in the form of original works can be seen as a far greater loss to humanity than the symbolic burning of a mass-produced and readily available volume. For this reason, the burning of a religious manuscript today is seen as an act of expression protected under the First Amendment. That would not be the case, however, with valuable original artifacts such as the Declaration of Independence and Emancipation Proclamation in the United States National Archives.

Over the last few weeks, religious tolerance in Egypt is facing one of its most trying times since President Anwar al-Sadat's heavy-handed stance and actions toward the Copts and the Church. The story of a once-estranged priest's wife, Camilia, has galvanized the public and polarized religious communities. Conflicting stories about her alleged conversion to Islam and her return to the Church has raised questions about apostasy and religious freedom. A fringe group of Azhari clerics that go by the name "al-Azhar Scientific Front" has called for a boycott of all Christian or Christian-majority establishments as a protest against what they believe is the Church's abduction of Camilia and forced conversion back to Christianity. Demonstrations against the pope and Church drew hundreds, particularly after some of the Egyptian press published photographs of Camilia in garb that resembles a veil, thereby suggesting she had converted to Islam. Protesters called on government authorities to interfere in what they believed to be the Church's supra-state powers and to make one of the world's oldest church authorities subservient to the state. Such a proposition was brought up in an interview with Father Bishoy, secretary for the Coptic Ecclesiastical Council, who responded in less than diplomatic terms, saying he is prepared for martyrdom to protect the Church's principles and describing the Muslim majority as once visitors to a nation of Coptic natives who welcomed them with open arms. At one point Bishoy expresses his dismay with the journalist's question, "What more do you want? You want to lead our prayers and run our church services too?"

Historically, church figures in Egypt rarely lose their cool the way Father Bishoy did, just as it is uncommon for a group of Azharis to refer to the pope as a "devil." These are unlikely and uncommon scenarios because they defy the pragmatic interests of both religious communities and constitute a blemish on the face of the fragile discourse of national unity. What would precipitate the publicization and mediatization of such intolerant discourses? In a nation whose media are still closely monitored and controlled, it comes as a surprise that the issue of Camilia's faith receives this much press attention despite the fact that all Coptic matters are considered very sensitive issues. Has the valve been opened to allow for this fodder to seep into public discourse? Why is the state surprisingly silent in the resolution of this issue? Perhaps there are larger political ends for this cacophony. It is well known that at times of sectarian strife, the Church and its adherents turn to the state for protection against the masses. In this case the regime has certainly won points with the Copts. Father Bishoy is not shy about expressing his affection for President Hosni Mubarak and his son Gamal in the very same interview. Conversely, the al-Azhar Scientific Front, a group usually at odds with the regime, is effectively appealing that the constitution be used by the state to control the Church. So in essence, on both accounts, the NDP comes out the victor. They may have even pulled the rug from underneath Mohamed ElBaradei's coalition by attracting both Copts and more conservative Muslim groups. But in the process they allowed intolerance to fester unabated between brethren.

At the end of the day, nations should be judged not by how they represent their majorities but how they treat their minorities. It is necessary for Egyptian Muslims not to perceive Christians as adversaries. It is also imperative that the topic of conversion be addressed comprehensively and in an egalitarian fashion to avoid these dangerously explosive scenarios. Fundamentally, the case of an individual woman's freedom of religion, not unlike the call for burning the Qur'an by a minuscule church in the United States, is a tempest in a teacup, telescopically magnified by the media with deplorable effects. Reality is lost in the midst of a vortex of media messages, emotions, and collective identification. So where is the reality?

French sociologist and cultural theorist Jean Baudrillard argued that in our era all realities are questionable, since all representations are manufactured. He used the term 'simulacrum,' Latin for 'likeness' or 'similarity,' to describe the copying or counterfeiting of realities. Not unlike reproduced paintings and photocopied manuscripts, a simulacrum fills in for the authentic reality. However, Baudrillard took the concept further by stating that today's simulacrum is unique in that the object it is meant to represent doesn't actually exist but rather "bears no relation to any reality whatsoever." In a world where media practices are capable of amplifying and magnifying happenings, the simulacra of reality replace the reality.

The Florida pastor Terry Jones's publicized intent to hold Qur'an burnings on September 11 is a good example of a simulacrum. Once the desire was expressed, the entire mechanism to document and manufacture the story of the burning and its repercussions was triggered and could not be stopped. In the end, as the pastor retracted his call for the Qur'an burnings, all that remained were hundreds of journalists convened on September 11 in front of the lawn of the Gainesville, Florida church to report nothing whatsoever.

Nevertheless, hyperreality had already been created. The virtual world of social media—blogging, Facebook, Twitter, and discussion forums— was alight with activity surrounding the public burning as if it had already happened. News stories about the burning had to be modified slightly but went to print to report nothing. People had already lost their lives defending the Qur'an from desecration. Afghan and Kashmiri demonstrations left sixteen protesters dead. But there were no Qur'ans burned. A non-event had stolen the spotlight on September 11.

What we must realize, however, is that in a world of infotainment and simulacra, where representation rules reality, unlike the time of Savonarola, it should be inconsequential when an unknown pastor calls for a Qur'an burning and what Camilia believes in her heart.

Learning to Mourn with the Poles

November 11, 2010

I t was a few minutes before noon on a chilly November morning when the professors and students from every department at the university, from mining to history, slowly filed into the majestically ornate Room 66 of the administration building. They had been asked to convene to attend a critical lecture about the overhaul of their institution of higher learning—among the most prestigious in the land. Their country, now under an occupying force, was about to undergo a forced ideological and cultural transformation and the new rulers declared the national education system was to be scrapped and replaced with their own.

Anxiety about how a change in the curriculum would affect the university was palpable and the scholars feared their jobs and careers might be in jeopardy. As the campus's 144 faculty and their assistants and students took their seats, and after a few minutes had passed, it became apparent that there was no speaker and no lecture to be delivered. The rector's mandatory invitation to the entire university to attend this lecture was a trap.

As members of a military known for its merciless brutality entered the room, it was evident something had gone eerily wrong. For the next half hour the building was filled with screams, shrills, and tears as the men in uniform arrested all the attendees on the pretext that the university was operating without the authorization of the new government. In a remarkably efficient act of intellectual annihilation, and in less than an hour, the country's oldest university, dating back to the fourteenth century, had been completely dismantled.

This is the story of Jagiellonian University in Krakow, Poland, which, on November 6, 1939, two months after the Nazi invasion of the country, ceased to exist. At the end of the incident, 184 members of the university community were arrested and deported to concentration camps in Sachsenhausen, Dachau, Auschwitz, and others, where thirty-four lost their lives and the rest were scarred by the torture they experienced and the horror they witnessed.

This incident in Krakow was repeated all over the country in an operation known as AB-Aktion (Ausserordentliche Befriedungsaktion), or Extraordinary Pacification Action, which was devised to eliminate the intellectual class in Polish society. In all, sixty thousand leaders, professors, teachers, aristocrats, artists, and priests were arrested or executed at ten regional sites during the Nazi control of Poland.

Every year on November 1–2 (All Saints Day/Day of the Dead), Poles lay wreaths and light candles on the graves and other spots commemorating their dead. During those days, the country is covered with flowers and candles, especially in Krakow, the regional capital of Nazi rule and a main artery in an extensive network of concentration camps. Auschwitz lies just sixty kilometers from the city. Over the past week, flowers sat in front of Room 66 of Jagiellonian University's main building to remind the academic community of what it sacrificed seventy-one years ago.

I often ask the Poles I meet about their collective psyche. How do they deal with loss and mourn death? How do they repent from guilt? How do they overcome trauma? Some say the Poles have developed an aesthetic appreciation and acceptance of somberness and melancholy. Others say that despite their pride as a nation, they have a strong sense of responsibility, bordering on self-deprecation. While Americans celebrate the day of the dead in the provocative, seductive, and absurd costumed festivities of Halloween, the Poles visit their family graves. Americans have a remorseless and unending "pursuit of happiness" that attempts to obscure the sadness of loss and replaces it with the mimicry of fantasy. The Poles engage with mortality and do not fear the somber contemplation of loss. It is not surprising, given the millions of people killed in cold blood in their land.

Yet most countries are following America's example—a nation where dire political circumstances are dominated more by farce than fact, where it is easier to distract than interact. It is not surprising that the largest political demonstration in Washington, D.C. this year was a faux protest called by a political satirist (Jon Stewart) and a parody of a right-wing pundit (Stephen Colbert) on Halloween weekend at a time of overwhelming duress in the American polity.

In our increasingly high-tempo, consumerist lives where we are often inundated by a seemingly infinite number of distractions, we are less inclined to deal with the unpleasant, the grotesque, and the deeply moving. Instead, we lead lives chasing after gratifications. We do not know or care to understand where our garbage goes; we have a narrowing patience for human tragedy; we are disgusted by the processes that bring food to our table; we are increasingly intolerant of aging; we go to great lengths to escape the specters of illness and try to abbreviate the mourning of death. How, then, do we deal with trauma if we spend much of our lives avoiding it in every small way?

Dealing with trauma is about exploring and rearticulating histories and truths. In Egypt we have a precarious relationship with truth. For those with the luxury of camouflaging their woes and escaping their responsibilities to society, their blindness to reality around them has created novel ways of seeing the world. But for many the dire reality is inescapable. It lives in every alley, yells from every rooftop, and sleeps in every shallow grave.

How do we deal with unpleasant realities and dark histories? How do we deal with the poverty that surrounds us? How do we confront our complicity in the living conditions of the Gazans? How do we come to terms with our exaggerated historical narratives, like that of our victory in the October 1973 War? How do we begin to address, and whom do we hold responsible for, the systematic decline of Egypt's intellectual class from the early days of the 1952 coup until today?

As controversial and problematic as these are, they are infinitely less burdensome than the guilt that the Poles continue to shoulder. Although they are the ones who suffered under Nazi occupation, they too have to live with the burden of these genocides. While we may not have participated in, condoned, or sat silent during the mass extermination of millions in our backyards, we too have skeletons in our closet, the kind that no Halloween costume can obscure. And while we continue to ignore the symptoms of the gaping wound in our collective consciousness, we go on like the living dead, sleepwalking in a seemingly consequence-free environment. But we must heed the impending revisionist history of our current day, which no measure of propaganda, laziness, or distraction can efface. Let us take a page from the proudly self-critical Poles by counting our losses, accepting defeat, admitting mistakes, repenting, and atoning for our hand in tragedy, and block out the careless chorus of inchoate optimism that has left us with few alternatives, and even fewer intellectuals.

Never Say No to the Panda

October 14, 2010

A characteristic of a global hegemon is its ability to exert influence and control beyond its geographic borders and natural proximities. America's role in the second half of the twentieth century exemplifies this characteristic. A multi-site realist approach produced America's brutal domination of Central and South American politics in the 1970s and 1980s, its economic mandates over Western Europe in the post–Second World War period, its stubborn foothold in Southeast Asia in the 1960s and 1970s following the Korean and Vietnam wars, and its expansion-by-proxy in the Middle East through unflinching support for Israel and corrupt dictatorships.

Since the collapse of the Soviet Union, America's insatiable pursuit of an adversary has left it spatting and sparring with real and perceived threats expressed through a paranoid fear of its declining power in the world. Over the past ten years, America's hard-talking competitiveness has resulted in periods of friction with virtually all secondary powers in the world—including Russia, India, Brazil, China, Iran, and Venezuela.

While the United States defined the direction of global politics and economics between 1990 and 2001, the gradually debilitating recession and two crippling wars in Afghanistan and Iraq seem to have overstretched its resources.

Behind the headlines, however, another superpower has risen to take America's place as the new global hegemon. Despite its abhorrent human rights record, its notorious inability to communicate across cultural divides, its bloated bureaucracy, its muted public sphere, its insular propagandizing, its weak 'public diplomacy,' and its limited appeal to the world at large, China has gone global. Today, no one in their right mind can ignore China's competitiveness in every global economic and political sector and its firm grip on international markets.

Liu Kang, a professor of cultural studies at Pennsylvania State University and author of Globalization and Cultural Trends in China, argues that what we see as a new global China is not novel. It is the result of a longstanding policy of *gaige kaifang* (reform and opening up) and not necessarily exclusive to a post-revolutionary Chinese culture.

As early as 1978, the Chinese government decided to begin experimenting with models of limited capitalism in specialized economic zones that were sealed from the rest of the country and where passport-controlled customs were imposed. Each of these zones had strong international trade connections with a diasporic Chinese community, such as Taiwan or Hong Kong. John Jirik, professor of journalism and communications at Lehigh University and a China specialist, argues that by 1992, Chinese leader Deng Xiaoping had been impressed by these zones and decided to expand them everywhere. Jirik explains that "industries were built across the country and eighteen years later, China has become the world's factory."

The hybrid communist-limited free-market model that China is using to access global markets may be an alternative model for modernization. But nevertheless, China can continue to present itself as a 'benevolent hegemon' to postcolonial nations that are wary of western-style neoliberalism. Instead, the Chinese can utilize another discourse of 'socialist anti-imperial solidarity' with countries in the Middle East, Africa, and South America.

Yet this discourse can often obfuscate the hard fact that China is no less a realist entity than the United States. The University of Georgia researcher Clifton Pannell argues that one of two characteristics of China's economic expansion into countries like Egypt, Iran, Sudan, South Africa, and Nigeria is the pursuit of raw materials and consumer markets for their cheap products. In countries like Ethiopia and Sudan, Chinese incentives are evident from a symbiotic trade environment for raw materials and infrastructural returns. Yet in Egypt, a country itself starved for natural resources, with weakening industries, minuscule reserves of raw materials, and a growing lower class, China can effectively flood the market with cheap consumer products. And it has.

Many have argued that while the complaints against dependence on the nexus of the United States Agency for International Development, the World Trade Organization, the International Monetary Fund (IMF), and the World Bank pose a threat to local industries, so has the Chinese alternative. In some quarters of the Egyptian market, everything from local pharaonic artifacts to Ramadan lanterns is being customized and manufactured in China for Egyptian vendors at a fraction of the local handicraft's cost (this year Ramadan lanterns were fashioned after Egyptian football star Muhammad Abu Treka and coach Hassan Shehata). The dilemma for Egyptian industries, as is the case in most countries, is whether host-country manufacturing can actually compete with the tidal wave of Chinese consumer products.

So at the end of the day, China has benefited from IMF and World Bank deregulation programs in Egypt and other emerging economies worldwide, and perhaps more so than anyone else. They have essentially beaten the United States and Western Europe at their own game. And this trend shows no sign of abating. With educated, disciplined laborers, China has at any moment close to 400 million people who are members of a cheap floating workforce. Whether they are making Ramadan lanterns for Egyptian football revelers or building a thirty-mile bridge connecting Hong Kong, Zhuhai, and Macao, the personnel behind China's international trade model are adaptable and mobile. Hence the scope of China's global influence, while seemingly invisible, is colossal, to say the least.

And invisibility has been a key characteristic of Chinese success. Unlike the abrasive in-your-face jingoism of American consumerism, China is content with flying under the radar. From the easily removable sticky tags that read "Made in China" on all products to their cultural and linguistic mimicking, this is a country content with being unbranded or counter-branded to avoid backlash. Given consumers' judgmental nature, camouflaging its national brand may be China's greatest export success. The Bahrain-based scholar Mohamed M. Mostafa documents this in a recently published study of animosity toward foreign products in Egypt. His structural equation model showed that consumer ethnocentrism and animosity toward the manufacturing country is a major factor in many Egyptians' decisions to purchase. His study focused on the immensely unpopular Israeli products.

Chinese products, however, have a different resonance in Egypt. Some perceive their 'Chineseness' as signs of shoddily made, short-lived, inferior, and perhaps even dangerous products (such as appliances, trinkets, and children's toys), while others are seen as efficient, affordable, and lean products, such as the omnipresent Speranza car. Yet regardless of perception, the breadth of imports from China in Egypt will necessitate a dependency, particularly in light of the dire economic conditions, for the majority of Egyptians today.

With each passing year under the IMF-imposed structural adjustment reforms, Egypt loses any competitive advantage it may have had—both agriculturally and industrially. As the country becomes increasingly dependent on imported goods, thereby forgoing its self-sufficiency and economic sovereignty, it succumbs to any and all hegemons in the international economic system. Given China's rising interests in the region and booming economy, it comes as no surprise to anyone that the Asian nation has great ambitions in Egypt.

On a not-so-unrelated note, there is a seemingly sarcastic and ironic metaphor for Egypt's growing dependence on Chinese products. The Egyptian cheese company, Panda, uses China's iconic endangered mammal to advertise its local iterations of Italian cheeses. In a series of commercials that have gone viral on YouTube, a serene-looking panda stands before all those who refuse to eat his brand of cheese, to the soothing background tune of Buddy Holly's "True Love Ways." The panda punishes the offenders by erupting in fits of violence where he destroys desk computers, knocks over shopping carts, ruins a cheeseless pizza, and even unplugs a sick person's intravenous drip. After the panda has exacted its revenge on all those who refuse its cheese, the ads close with the blatant warning, "Never say 'no' to the Panda."

Whether it is seen as cute, appealing, and delicious or ominous, creepy, and insidious, Egyptians are well on their way to accepting the Panda's hegemony.

Best in Show

November 25, 2010

E lections have always been more about performance than reality. Even in countries where public opinion informs and sways election outcomes, image is everything. In the United States, Barack Obama's Democrats were dealt a heavy election blow earlier this month because the White House and the president's party were unable to rebuff a public image of ineffectiveness and inactivity despite passing more significant bills than his immediate predecessor—from stem cell research to healthcare reform. Alternatively, one prospective Senate Republican candidate from Nevada, Sue Lowden, was defeated in the primaries when a candid comment she made about poor families exchanging chickens for medical services at doctors' offices was featured in a music video that ridiculed and scandalized her. Most of these successes and blunders in image management exist in a highly competitive field not monopolized by a single voice (but rather two).

The legitimacy of the American elections is embedded in the ability of the state to convince its public that the elections are competitive. Despite the egregious blemishes in the American "democratic" system, generally speaking, the national populace in the United States is sold on the theatrics of elections. In Egypt, efforts to persuade the public into believing that the elections to take place in a few days will be competitive, or representative of collective will, have fallen completely flat.

Since 2005, Egyptian elections have been marred with more than just violence. As the country has grown increasingly acquainted with seemingly competitive political contests, the majority of which have yielded the same results with only minor victories for any opposition group, it is evident to almost all opposition parties in this election that this is a competition between the sanctioned groups. Not only are most alternatives to the National Democratic Party (NDP) too embattled to compete on a level playing field, the field itself is rife with obstacles for any party hoping to contest the NDP's hegemony. Of the parties that decided to participate, most are now heavily disadvantaged due to intimidation, silencing, and in the case of the Muslim Brotherhood, waves of arrests. The climate in Egypt is not conducive to civic participation in this election and few believe that the public can avoid being thwarted again in what most observers expect to be a staged performance. So what is the point of voting?

What about the alternative to voting? Can the electoral or political systems be reformed by a boycott? The boycotts called for by several political blocs should not be judged by their effectiveness in reforming the political system or the electoral process. Instead their intention is to draw attention to the illegitimacy of the election structure itself. Knowing that the electoral process heavily disadvantages them, some of the opposition groups have decided to sit this one out. Of course the regime claims that this boycott is indicative of the inability of these groups to field candidates with any following and shows how empty and vacuous their platforms are. At the end of the day, these groups hope that by not participating they can delegitimize the elections, showcase their farcical nature, and not end up losing their traction as viable alternatives to the NDP if the elections had been free and transparent. So they may not be effective at reforming the electoral process, but they may undermine their results and highlight their defects.

Every good election performance needs an audience. Once again, the regime has decided that few would watch the final cut; the rest should be content with just the trailer. The procedures in the monitoring of this election are embarrassing, if not catastrophic. The monitors are not impartial. Many civil society groups have been denied monitor status without justifiable reason and the rules governing their work do not meet international standards. In fact, just two days ago, al-Sayyid Abd al-Aziz, the head of the High Elections Commission (HEC), declared that "authorized" civil society groups cannot "monitor" the elections but rather simply "follow" them. So yes, they will be able to do their job if that job is primarily to turn a blind eye to the obvious blemishes in the Egyptian elections.

In previous elections, the degree of irregularity has been astounding—from preventing members of the public from accessing the voting stations, to the ruling party paying off voters, to busing them en masse to the stations, to outright ballot stuffing. All of these have been documented meticulously by individuals and human-rights groups. So this may not be a new show audiences will be missing, but rather a tired and redundant replay of a less-than-captivating classic film, where the protagonist always prevails unanimously in an uneven contest.

Despite the overwhelmingly large backstage curtain that shields people's concerns from the political process, we can still hear the cacophonous voice of an Egyptian people. Their issues are simple and urgent—such as food, water, and electricity. The election is coming on the heels of one of the most miserable Eid al-Adha seasons in recent memory. At a time when animals are sacrificed for communal consumption, few can afford to eat them this holiday season—to the extent that some candidates running in the election were wooing voters by offering them meat. So while these are the matters occupying the average Egyptian's thoughts, they are anything but the agendas on the table in this election.

These elections should be a referendum on the disparities between rich and poor. It should be an opportunity to revisit the hyperbolic discourse about Egypt's record-breaking economic progress. The glowing economic and financial indicators that minister of finance Youssef Boutros Ghali praises include "direct foreign investment," but neglect other indicators such as hunger, rising unemployment, and average cost of living, which are not factored into these calculations. The economic progress they speak of is the dominion of a cadre of wealthy elite, not the masses who have yet to reap the benefits of the billions in economic growth the government is so swift to take credit for. So as the NDP unveils the same production of years past, Egypt looks mighty good on paper, but it is wilting from within. It is time we see past the glossy trailer and watch the grainy, gritty full feature. We owe it to the masses of the disenchanted who take to the streets every day to express their dismay and desperation.

Sadly, 144 years since the creation of the Egyptian parliament, we listen with earplugs in, we monitor with blindfolds on, and we vote with our hands tied. Although we hope election day can prove us wrong and affirm our faith in the process and rule of law, until that happens we are all dressed up with nowhere to go.

The Hegemony of Sharks

December 9, 2010

T he NDP government refused to accept international election observers under the guise of intervention and meddling in domestic affairs. Instead it has described the skewed High Elections Commission as a trustworthy institution that can protect the sanctity of the electoral process. Yet, thanks to new media technology and plenty of concerned citizens who dutifully documented and disseminated evidence of ballot stuffing and other violations, we now know the election was anything but free and transparent.

The elections did highlight, however, the lengths to which the regime is able to deploy the nationalist card. Government statements like "We do not accept criticism from the United States" and "This is a violation of Egypt's sovereignty" are meant to conjure up anti-colonial sentiments that run deep among Egyptians. More important than their effectiveness is their political inconsistency. From what we learned through WikiLeaks, this is an Egyptian government that consults with and relies heavily on foreign support, advice, and endorsement. So what is this charade about the country's autonomy and sovereignty at threat? A rude and humbling awakening happened shortly after the elections when the very same authorities that rebuffed the international community welcomed in experts from the very same nation they had turned a cold shoulder to. A sharp-toothed aquatic creature that claimed the life of a seventy-year-old German tourist had the government fly in shark behaviorists from Florida to assess the situation and determine a course of action.

Presumably, the reason for our acceptance of foreign meddling in our marine issues is warranted by our unfamiliarity with this variety of underwater predators. The same is evidently not true of elections, which we have mastered through extensive experience. This highlights two endemic problems in Egypt's contemporary culture of power and influence. The first is the failure to acknowledge or reprimand mediocrity, and the second is a state of hypnosis that allows the public to overlook, ignore, or tolerate this phenomenon.

Let us start with the first problem. In the same week that the world watched Egypt reel from its faux elections, they also watched another Arab country with one-eightieth of Egypt's population and 7,500 years its junior triumph over the United States and other world nations to host the most popular sporting event on earth, the football World Cup, in 2022. Qatar, a nation that has been a thorn in the ruling NDP's side since the emergence of Al Jazeera, may have pulled some strings, undergone a facelift, covered some blemishes, and put on its most extravagant façade to convince delegates to look past the obvious choice of the United States and sidestep the charm of its sponsor and former president Bill Clinton. The committee's decision to grant the minuscule peninsular state the right to host the event makes it the first Arab, Muslim, and Middle Eastern country to do so.

However, to most Egyptians over the age of six, watching this news came with a little lamentation as they remembered May 15, 2004, the day their country awaited a similar decision as one of several nations bidding for the first World Cup to be held in Africa. In a contest primarily against South Africa and Morocco, and with $7 million spent on the campaign to put forth the best portfolio and pamper the committee, the self-proclaimed leader of Africa could not garner a single vote out of twenty-four. It was a bitter humiliation that led to the launch of an inconclusive investigation where no one was reprimanded. Mediocrity had escaped unscathed. In fact, it had triumphed.

Six years later, the architect of the bid, then-minister of youth Ali Eddin Hilal, now holds the prestigious position of media chief of the NDP, whose job it has been to sell these parliamentary elections. It is no wonder that neither Egyptians nor the world bought them. In a cloud of shame, he was replaced as youth czar by Anas al-Fiqi, whose equally uneventful tenure earned him a promotion to minister of information.

The second problem is the state of hypnosis that engulfs Egyptian public culture in the face of this mediocrity. Perhaps it is a function of the incapacitation of judicial institutions in the face of this pandemic. Perhaps it is the fear of standing upright and demanding accountability.

But more likely, it is what the Italian Marxist writer and philosopher Antonio Gramsci called hegemony.

Once a leader of the Italian Communist Party in the 1920s, Gramsci's fervent attack on Italian fascism led to his arrest and imprisonment throughout Benito Mussolini's reign until his death eleven years later. In his seminal collection of writings, *Prison Notebooks*, Gramsci describes the structure of capitalist society and its consumerist drive as well as a system of myth-making that allows the elite, the government, and the powerful to shroud societal inequity behind various illusions of their making.

In the United States, one such myth is that of the "American Dream," which allows the populace to believe that all are created equal, that all are afforded equitable opportunities, and that anyone is capable of rising up the socioeconomic ladder. Anecdotes, statistics, and exemplars are there to affirm this myth. From basketball star Michael Jordan to President Obama, rags-to-riches stories are served up to keep the public hypnotized to the deeply entrenched incongruence that leads to the incarceration of one in six African American men, leaves 45 million Americans without health insurance, and pushes many of the remaining descendants of the continent's natives onto casino reservations.

Hegemony is the very process designed to shield inequities. It makes obstacles to change seem insurmountable, thereby making consent the only viable option. And if dissent emerges, hegemony is there to justify the use of brute force to bring tranquillity back to the system. Hegemony is the mechanism that divorces the memory of Malcolm X from its revolutionary roots, tames and domesticates Martin Luther King Jr., and transforms aboriginal communities into the subjects of ornamental fascination.

In Egypt, the last two weeks have been at once a sweeping success for the political elite and a damning blow to their hegemonic structure in Egypt. With every WikiLeaks revelation, the shroud of invisibility wears away, exposing one calamity after the next, refuting one myth after another. Some might be just waking up from the hypnosis, some might feel too disenchanted to demand change, and some will pay a hefty price for dissenting. But in the end, all this dissipates when our primordial fear of a pearly-jawed fish resurfaces and the shrieks strike a cacophonously mind-numbing crescendo.

The End of Illegitimacy

December 23, 2010

The newborn boy, Adam, had barely let out his first cry after leaving his mother's womb when the firestorm began. News travels fast in the twenty-first century and the story of Adam's arrival was online minutes after birth. Photos of him flanked by rejoicing parents circulated in cyberspace. Facebook pages and blogs teemed with activity, leaving the parents little time to celebrate.

Adam's father is Mohamed Zidan, Egypt's national football team star. His mother is Stina Rohde, a young Danish lady and Zidan's long-time girlfriend. In Germany, where Zidan plays for the club Borussia Dortmund, news of the birth was greeted with the usual festive remarks, and congratulations from team and fans alike. The parents publicly celebrated as the footballer shamelessly referred to Stina as his "girlfriend." But back home, the word alone seemed to have opened the gates of hell. The innocuous reference to the German press could have cost Zidan fame and following in his country of birth, where such an admission is a declaration that the player had violated Islamic practice and social custom by having a child out of wedlock.

News coverage of Adam's birth reverberated differently in Egypt than in Europe as papers scrambled to find the "correct" terminology for the relationship between Zidan and Stina. Is she a girlfriend, a partner, a mate, or a fiancée? Connotations for each of these terms can make or break the public's perception in a country where obedience to religious custom is becoming a test of one's character and where loyalty is judged by abiding by prescribed rules. Were they sexually involved before marriage? Is Stina a Muslim? Was the child born out of wedlock? From German press accounts, Egyptians could only see Adam as an 'illegitimate' child.

Zidan had few courses of action to salvage his image in a country of increasing religiosity where responsibility for judging and subverting religious failings is borne by all. The only thing Egyptians wanted to hear was a tale to quench their curiosity and resolve their conflicting feelings. The footballer, who is notorious for his mischief and liberal lifestyle, passed the test with flying colors. He declared himself a devout and practicing Muslim, argued that he had married Stina according to Islamic law in 2006, and proclaimed that their sexual relationship and first-born child, Adam, were both appropriate on the basis of Islamic jurisprudence. In a single interview, he redeemed his image to a skeptical public. In fact, Zidan went even further by condemning German marriage laws as prohibitive because of their prenuptial clauses that financially privilege the wife. He used this rationale to explain why Stina remains his "girlfriend" to the German press. According to Zidan, all of Egypt can rest assured that Adam is a legitimate Muslim child born to a devout father who deserved sympathy for facing a draconian German legal system that undermined the man's marital rights.

Adam's birth could have opened a can of worms, but Zidan's fabled response sealed it shut before any of the pressing issues could be addressed. An opportunity was lost to discuss Egypt's truly controversial personal status laws, the interpretation and application of *shari'a* to marriage, the multiplicity of marital options including *'urfi* and *mut'a*, the skyrocketing rates of divorce, the growing ranks of unmarried women, the absence of civil marriage options, and the outrageous shame of 'illegitimacy.' All these issues were postponed until the next scandal.

News of an estranged Saudi princess trickled into the British press a couple days later. This time it was a Saudi royal who was granted asylum in the United Kingdom to avert execution after having given birth to a child out of wedlock to an Englishman while married, at the same time, in her home country of Saudi Arabia. The "adulterous" princess's nationality, status, and gender prevented the public from affording her the benefit of the doubt enjoyed by Zidan. Her status as a Muslim woman does not give her the right to polygamy, which allowed Zidan (according to his tale) to remain married to Stina while being engaged to the Egyptian actress Mai Ezzeldin. Unlike Muslim men, she has no right to divorce her marriage partner at will to pursue another relationship. And if she were to secure a divorce, she could not marry a non-Muslim man unless he converted. So while Zidan can in a moment brush away the label of 'illegitimate' from his son Adam, the Saudi woman's child will have to carry that label for much of his life. And while the child may have to remain anonymous, over the years, other similarly unfortunate children have not gone unnoticed.

History is replete with examples of notable illegitimates, from artists and musicians to actors and entertainment personalities. Italian painter and mathematician Leonardo da Vinci, whose masterpieces include the *Mona Lisa*, *The Birth of Adam*, *The Last Supper*, and *Vitruvian Man*, was born out of wedlock. Television hostess and media mogul Oprah Winfrey was born to a poor single teenage mother in rural Mississippi. The ranks of human-rights advocates are filled with those who would otherwise be seen as the fruit of 'unbecoming' acts. Among them is African American abolitionist Frederick Douglass, one of the most renowned and accomplished black orators, who fought against slavery and wrote the seminal 1845 text *Narrative of the Life of Frederick Douglass, an American Slave*. Booker T. Washington was an African American educator born to a white father he knew nothing about and an enslaved black woman at a Virginia plantation. He grew up to become one of the most prominent black statesmen in America at the turn of the twentieth century.

Many a ruler and revolutionary was conceived under questionable circumstances. Fidel Castro, the Cuban revolutionary leader and former president, was born to a household servant and her prosperous Galician master. Others born under dubious circumstances include Alexander Hamilton, an economist, political philosopher, and one of America's founding fathers, who held the position of secretary of the treasury and drafted the *Federalist Papers*, which formed the foundations of the U.S. constitution.

America's third president and the main author of the 1776 Declaration of Independence himself fathered an illegitimate child with one of his slaves. The same is true of Albert Einstein, who fathered his first child, Lieserl, before marriage. Even Lawrence of Arabia was born out of wedlock, to an Irish baronet and his own daughter's governess.

Famed novelist and playwright Alexandre Dumas, author of French classics such as *The Count of Monte Cristo* and *The Three Musketeers*, as well as his countryman Jean Genet, were born out of wedlock. Even the early-sixteenth-century Catholic pope Clement VII of the famed Florentine Medici family had an ambiguous birth record. But none had to battle the label of 'illegitimate' more than William the Conqueror, the first Norman king of England, who annexed the country in 1066. Known to his adversaries as "William the Bastard," his illegitimacy affected his early life—from assassination attempts in hope of preventing his coronation to incessant taunts by his nemeses.

Illegitimacy has been a source of fascination for literary giants such as William Shakespeare, Charles Dickens, and Leo Tolstoy. In Dickens's *Bleak House*, the heroine and narrator of the story, Esther Summerson, is illegitimate but raised as an orphan. The discovery of her illegitimacy is the crux of the story, and Dickens ensures that, while she may have been born of 'sin,' she embodies the heart of morality.

Unlike the time of Dickens, today bearing and rearing children outside of the traditional institutions of marriage is on the rise worldwide. In the United States last year, the National Center for Health Statistics announced that nearly 40 percent of babies born in the country in 2007 were delivered by unwed mothers (1.7 million out of 4.3 million total births), a 25 percent increase from five years earlier. European figures are even more staggering, as more than half of all births in many countries, including France, the United Kingdom, the Netherlands, Denmark, Austria, the Czech Republic, and throughout Scandinavia, occur out of wedlock. The frequency of births outside of marriage has resulted in a shifting perception of 'illegitimacy.' Even language is being overhauled to reflect a de-stigmatized view of these births. In many countries, where such births constitute a significant percentage of total births, the term 'illegitimate' has been replaced by 'natural child' and 'out of wedlock.'

The rise of illegitimacy is also evident in much of the Arab world. Statistics are hard to come by because most illegitimate children are either camouflaged and assimilated by their families to avoid public shame, end up without paperwork (hence outside the state's purview), or find their way to orphanages where they become invisible among those whose parents have died. Nevertheless, few Arab government entities are prepared to release studies examining the extent of the problem for fear of national dishonor. The Algerian Ministry of National Cooperation, one of the more transparent institutions in the region, announced that between 1,100 and 1,200 illegitimate children are born every year in Algeria.

In other Arab countries facing military conflicts, such as Iraq, Sudan, and Somalia, the increasing incidence of rape, sexual slavery, forced prostitution, and forced marriage has led to spikes in unwanted pregnancies. During wars, women are often forced to offer sex for survival, food, shelter, or protection, all contributing to a rise in the number of illegitimate children.

Today, Egyptian orphanages are filled with more children abandoned by their parents than children orphaned by their parents' death. The act of disownment is often a result of anxiety about judgment by society, culture, religion, and the law. Many children are placed in the garbage or left at the doors of mosques, churches, and orphanages due to paranoia about Egyptian law and the desire to avoid social stigma, shame, and fear of retribution. These children have been the subject of many literary and cinematic productions, including Khaled Yousef's film *Hina maysara* (Until Better Days).

Most attempts to reduce illegitimacy rates in Egypt focus on invigorating religious teachings and prohibiting gender mixing. Grand Mufti Ali Gomaa has argued that illegitimacy, premarital relations, and challenges to traditional marriage can be averted by increasing polygamy. This is an impractical approach that does not address the conditions and lived experiences of illegitimacy. We need civic, not religious, solutions to this problem. We need solutions that unravel patriarchy, not entrench it. We need solutions that help integrate those who are different, rather than continuing to exclude them. We must tackle the economic disparities that have redrawn Egypt's marital patterns.

Despite the overwhelming social and religious barriers to change, the last few years have witnessed the emergence of new laws, albeit at a sluggish pace, to improve the fortunes and livelihoods of these children. One law came after the highly public saga involving the paternity of the once little-known costume designer Hind al-Hinnawi's illegitimate child with actor Ahmad al-Fishawi. While in the past only a father could sign a birth certificate, the amendment enables a mother alone to sign it for her child. Prior to the law, there was an exponential rise in the number of children admitted to orphanages and living on the streets. However, much still remains to be accomplished.

The tens of thousands of Egyptians who were born out of wedlock, mostly away from the public eye, deserve a measure of dignity that starts with the obliteration of the very notion of 'illegitimacy.' Let us use this term in its rightful legal context, reserve it to describe what is unlawful in the eyes of social, economic, and political justice, and resign it from undermining those born pure. If they are given their rightful place in society, Egypt may find among those legitimate children its own da Vinci or Genet.

Coptic Exodus from Disneyland

January 6, 2011

For decades, Egypt's Copts have found a safe, comfortable, and joyous haven in the one place where dreams come true, where good always triumphs over evil, where justice is universal, and where all things negative can be banished with the rub of a lamp or a wave from a wand.

The imaginary world of Disneyland has been a home for the Copts at least since the mid-1950s following the coup that overthrew the monarchy and ended the British colonial presence in Egypt. From that point forth, the discourse of national unity between Muslims and Christians became a façade for state policy. But Disneyland has a way of twisting stories to make them more palatable, agreeable, and friendly. For instance, the story of Cinderella, a German fable collected by the nineteenth-century brothers Jacob and Wilhelm Grimm, described the stepsisters trying to deceive the prince in his search for his love by cutting off parts of their feet to get the slippers to fit. Disney's retelling of the story of Peter Pan was also lightened up significantly from its early script by Scottish playwright J.M. Barrie, omitting any tragic incidents. In the original story, Neverland (actually London's Kensington Gardens) is where the heartbroken Peter Pan lives. He has missed his childhood and cannot relate to kids. When Peter isn't playing, he is busy building graves for the children who get lost in the night, burying them in the garden under little headstones—certainly not the exuberant tale of festive nighttime escapades across distant lands that presides in Disneyland.

Just like Peter Pan and Cinderella, the Copts too have their own fairytale story in Disneyland, a story that has been embellished for maximum gratification, amusement, and delusion. The fable of interfaith harmony where Coptic rights are respected, their civility acknowledged, their rituals tolerated, and their identities celebrated has stood its ground for many years and even has its own mascot. Like Disney's Mickey Mouse ears, 'the crescent and the cross' has served as the unified national logo of Coptic utopia, affirming the commitment of all members of Egyptian society, officials and citizens, to equality under the law. Any attempts to call this myth into question are barred completely.

Last year at a conference at Durham University in the United Kingdom, I spoke about Copts and language. Following my presentation, an Egyptian colleague expressed his reservations about my discussion and argued there was no such thing as Copts. Since the term itself was Greek for 'Egyptian,' he asserted that as an Egyptian Muslim, he too was technically a Copt. Of course, he was both well-meaning and etymologically correct. Yet by forcing his assertion of the inseparability of Muslim and Christian in Egypt, he effectively erased the latter. What his comment highlighted was a naïveté about an identity that has been in the making for over two thousand years. Fundamentally, denying someone's existence does little to empower them. Instead it is a dismissal of any case made by the Christian about any predicament that affects him due to his faith. One cannot make a case about something that doesn't exist. Donald Duck cannot sue someone for discriminating against talking birds.

A similar conversation happened exactly a year ago with a group of my Muslim friends about the Nag' Hammadi shooting. Trying to explain the grievances of the Coptic community to them, I was met with a combination of shock and disapproval. Any attempt to highlight the disenfranchisement of Copts is treated as if one were reiterating foreign imperial allegations, and is answered with such responses as "But my boss is a Copt," or "Sawiris is a Coptic success story in Egypt," and the always classic "But our economy is run by Copts, look at [finance minister] Youssef Boutros Ghali." The immunity of a few does not dismiss the plight of the many. The logic of these arguments resembles the polemic that writes off Islamophobia in the United States because President Barack Obama had a Muslim father or the reigning Miss USA Rima Fakih (2010) is Muslim. In reality, Copts are underrepresented in real life and fiction. Few notable athletes in Egypt's history have been Copts, and a dwindling number feature on the silver screen. Egyptian cinema rarely presents Christians, and when it does, they are often grossly caricatured. Nevertheless, there is a stubbornness to the discourse of national harmony.

While 'the crescent and the cross' may suggest equality, few Copts would attest to it behind closed doors. In fact, before the 1952 coup, Copts played an active and visible role in the nation's politics, comprising around 10 percent of the parliamentarians. Today that has dropped to a minuscule and negligible unofficial quota. In 2011, virtually no Copts are elected to political office. Those who serve in any governmental capacity are appointed by the president, largely to save face and demonstrate that the Christian minority has representation. The rest have simply resigned themselves to abandoning civic life. So politically speaking, there is barely a cross next to the crescent. Hence, the government has conditioned the Copts to understand that without the ruling NDP, they would have no political status, forcing them into complete allegiance and loyalty.

There is a mosque for every 770 Muslims in the country and those are just the ones registered by the state, not the makeshift structures that were converted into places of worship under the authorities' nose, most of which no Egyptian official in his right mind would dismantle. In fact, even public space in the country has been converted to a place of worship for the majority. It is not unusual to see entire hallways in government buildings and whole street blocks turned into communal prayer areas. So if Muslim worship is everywhere, where do Christians practice their faith? By contrast, there is a church for every 3,100 Christians in Egypt, and all have to be registered with the state and must have their papers in order or risk facing the same violent state intervention orders as the Umraniya case some weeks ago. All forms of prayer are performed inside the walls of churches, not outside them. So even in supplication to the same deity, the crescent's prominence is so vast it often overshadows the cross.

But it is the crimes against Copts that grab headlines and sour relations most. According to the Egyptian Initiative for Personal Rights, fifty-two anti-Christian incidents were reported between 2008 and 2010 and all have gone unpunished. These are not to be confused with incidents 'involving' Christians, but are what in other countries would be referred to as 'hate crimes.' It appears that while the government has punished the Islamic opposition over the years, it has also tolerated many of the fundamentalist groups that openly demonize Christianity and express disdain for the Copts. Today, a growing number of Egyptian Muslims feel they have more in common with Pakistani Muslims and German converts to Islam than they do with Christian Egyptians.

In many instances, the state has benefited from pitting Muslim and Christian against one another. By showing the Copts that radical Islam is on the rise in Egypt, the state asks for complete loyalty in return for promising Copts physical security at their places of worship, essentially making them clients to an unreliable and oppressive security apparatus. Over the past few years, the Copts have realized that the government has actually violated its long-standing agreement with them. It no longer protects them, supports their causes, or speaks to their interests. Hence, they have now taken the grave risk of no longer supporting the NDP and confronting the government's security, as is evident from the last few days of incessant furor against the police.

Many Muslims have hardly contemplated Coptic concerns before and are perplexed at the sight of enraged Christian youths on the streets. What they must know is that the Copts have been jarred and jerked out of a fifty-year snooze and are declaring at the top of their lungs: "Yes, there is a Coptic problem and it needs to be resolved." These are not the diasporic Copts on whom we peg sectarian problems. These are the disgruntled Coptic youth of Egypt, from Sidi Bishr, Alexandria (the neighborhood of the Two Saints Church that was bombed a few days ago) to Luxor. Ignoring their anger, as opposed to addressing it, is itself a recipe for sectarianism.

Coptic expressions of dissent may be uncomfortable for many Muslims, but they should not be. When disenfranchised Muslim youths in Paris riot against marginalization or protest against a face veil ban, how do we view their dismay? Is it a threat to the delicate religious balance of France or a call for sectarianism? Unlikely. Instead, we see it as a civil rights movement demanding equality. Shut out from public life for decades, Copts have bottled up their aggravations and now emotions are boiling over. Muslims should not fear Coptic activism. It is not a threat to national unity and it is not a condemnation of Islam. Quite simply, it is a community in rage, and rightly so. Let them vent. Listen to their qualms. Understand their plight. Help them heal their wounds. Share their anger. Join the Facebook campaigns but go beyond their facelessness. Visit their churches. Dress in black on Friday. Think beyond condolences. And consider how Egypt can be more inclusive to them.

Many Muslims have already declared their solidarity with their Christian brethren, not just in their right to mourn and get angry, but in sharing their woes. Some have gone as far as deciding to go to the churches on Christmas Eve to act as human shields. These, along with the heartfelt condolences, are a major step toward healing the gaping wounds caused not by the tragic events of January 1, 2011, but rather by the decades of living in utopia. However, the real stand will come after the tears have been shed and the blood dried, when it is time to press for change in Egypt. This will start with acknowledging that Copts exist and have equal rights that must be protected, and that the state's ineptitude in determining its priorities vis-à-vis all its citizens will have grave consequences.

Sadly, evidence of this ineptitude still abounds. A heated exchange occurred in the Shura (Consultative) Council, the upper house of parliament, just a couple of days after the explosion at the Two Saints Church and with Coptic nerves boiling. Top state officials debated Tagammu' Party leader Rif'at al-Said regarding a unified law for building places of worship. While al-Said argued that it was time to finalize the law so as to make it comparable for all faiths, the top NDP brass responded that terrorism should not be an incentive to amend laws on mosque and church construction. What the NDP still fails to understand is that this has nothing to do with terrorism or the bombing, but rather the state's responsibility to provide equal rights for all its citizens. This blunder is a sign of blatant impunity and disregard for justice.

One upon a time, a pan-Arab ideology superseded and undermined factionalism in Egypt. Today, this has been replaced with an amalgam of contradictions—a schizophrenic state. Egypt is a nation for all faiths but Islam is the official religion. It is a republic but there is no true transition of government. It is an Arab nation but has largely disowned its commitments to Arab causes. It is civic yet doctrinal, and neoliberal yet illiberal. Perhaps out of this New Year's cataclysm, the nation may find its bearings and create a novel paradigm for a truly plural identity.

In the meantime, the same old tired slogan of 'the crescent and the cross' has been dusted off and used as an improvised emergency flag, waved only when fear of sectarian tension requires cosmetic concealment. We, Egyptians of all faiths and stripes, should insist and ensure that 'the crescent and the cross' not be evoked to uphold the status quo but rather, per its original and untarnished purpose in the 1919 revolution, to bring everyone together to advance along a new path. Let it be the symbol of a genuinely new Egypt, not the fantastical state-manufactured Disneyland that the Copts are now abandoning en masse.

Ablaze the Body Politic

January 20, 2011

T
he powers that be want us to be passive observers. And they
haven't given us any other options outside the occasional, purely
symbolic, participatory act of voting. You want the puppet on
the right or the puppet on the left?" The young man utters these words
angrily as he sits cross-legged on the sidewalk and douses himself with
gasoline. "I feel that the time has come to project my own inadequacies
and dissatisfactions into the sociopolitical and scientific schemes. Let my
own lack of a voice be heard." He lights a match and sets his body ablaze.

This is perhaps the most jarring scene from the exceptionally creative
animated film *Waking Life* by Richard Linklater, which offers a series of dizzyingly profound yet disconnected diatribes delivered by various characters
speaking to a confused but curious semi-conscious protagonist. This particular interaction is with the philosophical prototype of the self-destructive
man. The self-immolator describes this state as "completely alienated and
utterly alone." He is essentially "an outsider to the human community."

We have no qualms about condemning all those who inflict harm on
the bodies of others or destroy their lives. Tyrannical regimes that fire live
ammunition into the disgruntled unarmed bodies of demonstrators—
whether they be Tunisia's Zine El Abidine Ben Ali's police force, the Thai
government's security apparatus against the Red Shirts, or the Israeli
Defense Forces against Palestinians—often appear to have lost their moral
compass entirely in the eyes of outraged populaces. Other institutions
will subject the human body to unspeakable horror in the most abhorrent
manner to arrive at one end—complete submission. These are the institutions that leave behind long trails of victims—the likes of Khaled Said and
more recently Sayid Bilal, who appears to have died in police custody after

sustaining severe injuries during a session of torturous interrogations following the Alexandria church bombings.

In every case, it is the strong hand of the 'law' rehabilitating individuals into tacit acceptance of the way things are and into vowing complete cooperation. But in some instances, the shaky unsure hand that holds aloft the baton comes down too hard, crossing a very thin line and forcing a new relationship between the powerful and the powerless. With the final mortal breath, the victim is immediately transformed into the victor, and the omnipotent is rendered impotent. Recently, we have witnessed how a single foolish act that cost the life of the young man Khaled Said has spurred a movement in Egypt against torture and corruption. Once completely unknown to his fellow Egyptians, Said's name in death has become a rallying cry. And while his body is no longer among us, his two-dimensional image now possesses political capital, and his posthumous page has more supporters on Facebook than all Egyptian political figures combined.

In Tunisia an unlicensed vegetable vendor, Muhammad Bouazizi, joined the ranks of the few who self-immolated out of helplessness and anguish in what could have been a local incident. Bouazizi's action was a genuinely epic David-versus-Goliath scenario, where David liberated himself from the fear of persecution by destroying himself and laying Tunisia's corrupt and authoritarian political order naked for onlookers to see. The camouflage of power had been rendered obsolete and the injustice of the status quo was no longer unspoken.

We know that suicide today is one of the many ailments of our modern age. Hundreds of thousands of people from all walks of life, in all societies, classes, and races, decide to terminate their lives against all legal, social, and ethical norms. Principles and ideologies that look upon these actions favorably are often ostracized by mainstream society almost everywhere. Nevertheless, this admonishment does not take away from the fascination with what appears to be the most selfless act the human mind can conjure.

The body is the canvas on which we carve our identities, from prayer bumps on the forehead to Coptic crosses on the wrist, from the way we adorn it with accessories to what we choose to feed it or withhold from it. We reward and punish our bodies with frills and thrills. And while we largely believe it is our own to tamper with, a body in no small measure is also claimed by those who come into contact with it. Religious doctrine and social custom dictate how the body should be displayed and used, and we choose whether to conform to or revolt against these norms.

The body is also an important symbol of protest. One cannot underestimate the power of disfigured bodies to create outrage. Videos and images of Tunisian protesters' bullet-holed bodies and open skulls ignited more demonstrations. The photo of Khaled Said's contorted and lacerated face alone created a firestorm in Egypt and kick-started a movement.

And while the precedent has been set in Tunisia, and everyone stands still waiting for the quake to ripple elsewhere, there is no dearth of heroes prepared to be martyrs, desperate to taste a life of dignity. The half dozen people who have attempted to self-immolate and follow in the footsteps of Bouazizi in the hope that their brethren can lead better lives may be called copycats, but their plight is one.

As discussions reverberate worldwide on the nature of revolution in the wake of Tunisia, enthusiasts and skeptics stake their odds. Social psychologists will debate political scientists and anthropologists will argue with media scholars about the peculiarities of the Tunisian phenomenon. They will contest what compels people to self-mutilate, destroy their own bodies, or inflict unbearable pain on themselves with intent and design. They will argue why, day in and day out, thousands of protesters knowingly confronted a force that was prepared to murder them. They will argue every minuscule detail in the months and years to come. But they will all agree on one point—that the complicated arithmetic of revolution is actually a very straightforward equation. In societies where tyranny reigns supreme and does so with unimaginative blatancy, change is merely a question of will—the will to undertake a single political act of the body that can ignite a nation's body politic.

But first Arab publics must overcome their desensitization to human loss, their tacit acceptance of the pain of others, and their discrediting of those who sacrifice where they barely budge. They must go beyond uttering "ooohs" and "aaahs" at news of other people's sacrifices. Change is not a spectator sport that one buys tickets to watch. Arab publics must go beyond their necrophilia, which has left them enslaved voyeurs in their own lives, insatiably drawn to the agony of others. Rather than being captivated by the body counts on Al Jazeera tickers, they should make their own bodies count—not by setting their bodies ablaze but rather by being prepared to respond to the call of the body politic.

The Gravity of Pharaohs

January 28, 2011

The dizzyingly rapid demise of Mubarak's exceptionally stable regime is a surprise to even the most seasoned analysts and avid observers of Egypt. For all those who speculated that Egypt was not Tunisia, who paraded the notion that its populace was notoriously apathetic, that the Arab world's most populous nation had an aversion to revolution, or that the cowardly eighty-plus million had feared Mubarak more than their own starved bellies, the last couple of days have been a humbling time for those who offered such baseless prognostications.

The government, with its brutal and abhorrent actions against protests on January 25, has lost the last bit of legitimacy it may have possessed. The level of disrespect that the state has for its people is beyond caste-like. Treating its citizens as clients of its benevolent caretaking, it has managed them with impunity for generations. Hence, the level of violence should come as no surprise to anyone. Since 1973, the government has decided that by forgoing the possibility of war in the foreseeable future, its conscription would be steered toward building the largest police force in the region. Egypt effectively created an army whose sole task is to suppress, torture, subdue, and oppress its own people.

This configuration results in a government that constantly chases an opposition. The dissidents are the mice in a cat and mouse game. But on Tuesday, January 25, the Egyptian mouse woke up and looked itself in the mirror only to discover it is an elephant. In Egypt today, a large, amorphous, young, dynamic, diverse, multidenominational movement comprises practically every swath of the population, barring the few that benefit from the bloated kleptocracy. Instead the tables have turned and the colossus threatens to stamp out the paper tiger of the state.

As this article goes to press, the Egyptian abomination of a regime will have completely shut down all Internet access in the country and most telephone service, turning Egypt into a communication black hole—worse than North Korea. With the flip of a switch, the country's Internet Freedom Index went from 45 (o being totally free) to 100. The government broke world records in Internet censorship by creating an absurdly surreal situation. This shutting down of all forms of online communication amounts to the largest block in the history of the Internet.

Without knowing it, the Egyptians are testing Clay Shirky's theories on social networks, Mark Zuckerberg's claim of Facebook's power, the logic of Twitter revolutions, and YouTube's slogan of "Broadcast Yourself." The strength of the Internet generation is being tested to the absolute limit. Just minutes before the supposed eruption of the revolution that hopes to bring down the regime once and for all, the people, just a few days after feeling a true semblance of common destiny, are severed from one another. Not only is communication between them now a luxury, they are living on an isolated island—a fate not unlike that of Robinson Crusoe.

This makes Egypt the only true grounds for the ultimate test of all media-effect speculations, game theories, and social-movement hypotheses. Can a virtual revolution that germinated online overthrow a regime in the absence of the portal on which it was built? Can a generation trained to tweet their dissent function without their nifty gadgets? Can they trust one another's commitment to a common cause to go out into the eerily quiet streets of Egyptian cities and find their fellow compatriots also on hand to fulfill their destiny? Can they function as a network without an originator, organizer, and administrator?

Today is the beginning of a dream for generations of Egyptians. Regardless of the outcome in the coming hours, days, weeks, or months, history has indeed been made. Call it the Lotus Uprising, the Bread Intifada, or the Anger Revolution; clichés are inconsequential. What matters is that despite not being able to witness what is happening in Egypt now, we can be sure it is historic! Where this takes Egypt is of little consequence at this moment, for it has already delivered them from the abyss in just forty-eight hours. As the severity of the moment sends Egypt's last tyrant and his cronies into free fall, we must rest assured that a regime this irrational is a regime in eclipse. It should be drastically clear to anyone who once courted the Cairo felons that they must abandon ship now or risk losing any semblance of dignity.

Egypt's day of reckoning is upon us. Mubarak's government has committed major blunders in its almost three decades in power. But none will be more costly than its outrageously arcane and vulgar attempt to silence the whole nation. For a president who has flaunted himself as the advocate of free press and freedom of opinion, his government is now parading in the nude while hiding behind a media blackout. But this nudity cannot be concealed for long. Even a besieged, embattled, obliterated Gaza had its eyewitnesses, its cameras, and its Goldstones. The day of reckoning for the regime leaves it with little time to decide between two options: either to retract its stubbornness and make irreversible concessions to its people on matters that are inalienably rightful and unquestionably just, or consciously lay its own head on the guillotine and pull the cord.

It is clear that the regime will not go away of its own accord and will hang on by the skin of its teeth. But on January 25, Egypt's youth shattered the barriers of apathy, fear, and disregard, leaving Mubarak's circle toothless at the moment of their greatest challenge. And as Egyptians roar with anger and chant in unison the oft-repeated Tunisian slogan, "The people want the fall of the regime," Mubarak is holed up in an undisclosed location and utterly speechless. For a population so accustomed to his pontification on every occasion—from Army Day to visits from Monrovian ministers—a silent pharaoh is a fallen pharaoh. His people spent much of the first day of protests tearing down his image, desecrating his obelisks. And while he is so accustomed to arresting foreign perpetrators and banning opposition, today he has declared that all Egyptians are enemies and adversaries and is besieging them in their homes, in their country.

But he has only hurt himself. A regime that arrests and beats its own government media personnel is one that knows not its friend from its foe and has lost its bearings. But this may be because the regime has actually lost all of its friends. Mubarak has made it impossible for compatriots to remain steadfastly friendly. The U.S. State Department is trying to dodge the bullet by offering mixed signals to avoid a foot in the mouth, and may actually be recalculating what is in its national interests in the future. The least politicized of Egypt's elite came out in droves to the January 25 protests. And now with Facebook down, some 20 million Egyptian Internet addicts in the country have nothing further to distract them from revolting.

A new beginning became clear to me when I realized that the national paper *al-Ahram* ran a front-page story on the morning after Tuesday, January 25, describing citizens visiting police stations and giving officers flowers and chocolates on the occasion of Police Day. On a day that featured some of the most dramatic confrontations between the people and the police, a stock photo of the minister of torture Habib al-Adly and a clip-art drawing of a flower bouquet was a reminder that no such exchange had happened. And while the Egyptian people are accustomed to being lied to, on the second day, the people responded with fervor. The online comments under this story were exceptionally long and replete with admonishments against government propaganda and profanities against Mubarak and Company. This was not unlike Egyptian radio's Voice of the Arabs broadcast during the 1967 War, which reported victories against Israel while the country's military was virtually obliterated. But these matters are not unexpected. What is unexpected is to find myself unable to publish my own column in my newspaper, *Al-Masry Al-Youm*, because the Internet is cut off nationwide, leaving my editors stranded and unreachable.

Nevertheless, and despite the media blackout, let this week's events be a message to Mubarak's regime: virulence and victory rarely rendezvous. Pharaohs, too, eventually submit to gravity.

Dared to Defy

February 12, 2011

F ebruary 11, 2011 is a monumental day in history. The resilience and resolve of the Egyptian people have shown the world how a revolutionary movement can rise up to sweep away all that lies in its path and create a new reality. I understand this sounds like hyperbole, but the past two weeks were not exactly a time for conservative assessment.

With the resignation of Mubarak and the passing of all authority to the military, the people of Egypt have forced their will against all odds and in a manner quite unexpected to most prognosticators and analysts. The revolutionaries, from computer-savvy techies to bus drivers, and from housekeepers to engineers, defied colossal obstacles to achieve this decisive victory.

They defied a deeply entrenched and corrupt police system that was designed to dehumanize and instill fear in them. They defied thirty years of Emergency Law that refused them even their most inalienable rights. They defied competing intelligence agencies actively concocting ways to undermine any opposition. They defied systematic torture and brutality delivered by batons, tear gas, rubber bullets, live rounds, and whip-wielding camel riders.

The Egyptian revolution defied a matrix of regional political interests, from Israeli pressure and Saudi intransigence to U.S. equivocation. The unyielding strength of the protesters forced the U.S. administration to execute one of the most startling U-turns in diplomatic expression in many years. Secretary of state Hillary Clinton first stated that the Egyptian government was "stable" and vice president Joe Biden asserted that Mubarak was not a "dictator." The tone would change dramatically as the Egyptian people who poured into the streets and liberated Tahrir Square in their millions established new realities on the ground. For once, the Egyptian street, usually either ridiculed or lamented, erupted in a show of force unparalleled in the nation's history.

Most of all, the revolution defied definition. It was practically impossible to attribute the movement to any clear singular ideological thrust besides supporting freedom and social justice. The revolution was not advocating communism, nor was it pushing for further neoliberalization. It was neither an Islamic revolution nor a secular one. The infamous Muslim Brotherhood was neither a trendsetter nor absent in the revolution's development. Even the Iranian Republic, which saw an opportunity to benefit from the Egyptian revolution's criticism of American complicity, could not convince the revolutionaries or anyone else that this was an Islamic movement. The revolution continued despite the world conspiring against it. Only the Danish prime minister called for Mubarak to step down before the official announcement came through.

The Egyptian revolution may have trumped both journalist and writer Malcolm Gladwell's reluctant and depressing realism about the power of social media to create change and writer Clay Shirky's hyperactive enthusiasm and technological determinism. While the revolution may have been mobilized on Facebook and Twitter, it was sustained by millions who had never touched a computer in their lives. While it was the online activists that built communication bridges to the world, it was during the government-imposed five-day Internet blackout that the size of demonstrations swelled significantly.

This is a revolution that refuses to submit or conform to tradition and has resisted every kind of co-option or tarnishing. The protesters could not credibly be accused of being radical, foreign-trained operatives. They could not be accused of being unruly mobs of violent thugs. They could not be accused of being members of an indoctrinated group. Despite the regime's stubborn attempts to undermine the revolution, it remained largely faceless and universal.

Despite the role of Mohamed ElBaradei, opposition politician Ayman Nour, the Facebook superhero Wael Ghoneim, and other notables in fomenting support for the sustained demonstrations, the revolution asserted its independence, its democratic values, and its disinterest in the cult of megalomania. It became clear from the outset and remained the case throughout that this revolution wished to be independent from any political force that may hijack it, and undermined any glamorization of heroes and leaders. It is a revolution that seeks the support of the military but is opposed to military rule.

This revolution was started largely by a population that just a few weeks ago showed their solidarity with a simple 'like' on a Facebook page. Today they have become the nucleus of a powerful movement that has shattered all barriers before the Egyptian people, forcing even the most powerful institutions to buckle at a name like Khaled Said. In just seventeen days, the Egyptian revolution defied everything from tyranny and imperialism to patriarchy, tribalism, sexism, and ageism.

It even defied the natural order of revolutions. At its height, it did not attempt to take over the main institutions of government and assert its triumph over the state. Rather, it simply asserted the stubbornness of human perseverance and liberty in the face of unbearable pain and agony. It did not try to undo the constitutional order with disorder, but rather respected the need to demand change and expected that its show of force would be enough to guarantee the legitimacy of these demands. It ebbed and flowed from crescendo to trough, with every call to action from the youth and every demoralizing and condescending speech from Mubarak and other government officials. The world has swayed back and forth with the protesters, each time taking a deep breath before each day of rage, redemption, departure, and march of millions.

Whether you view it through anecdotes and testimonies or through the mind-boggling numbers of protesters, the story of the Egyptian revolution is exceptional. The number of demonstrators in Cairo alone exceeded a million on more than three occasions, and the total number of protesters across the country may have reached eight million on one occasion—10 percent of the population. These are numbers that eclipse both the French and the Russian revolutions. The story of the revolution is a colossal media story. It is Hurricane Katrina, the Chilean miners, and the fall of the Berlin Wall all in one incredible amalgam of intrigue that reaffirms the triumph of humanity.

For more than two weeks, we have listened to reluctant skeptics comment about the unlikelihood of this day, but, alas, it has come. They must admit their egregious failure to predict one of the largest popular uprisings in history. They must admit they underestimated the most exuberant manifestation of the long-clichéd notion of 'people power' in our lifetime. The Egyptian revolution has humbled many an analyst and inspired many an observer. From learned academics to leaders of global superpowers, all have had to mince their words for fear that their prophecies may falter. Egypt has resuscitated the utility of civil disobedience and revived the old, once-tired mantra of "*Viva la revolución.*"

2

REVOLUTION INTERRUPTED?

Nor will there ever be wanting to a prince legitimate reasons to excuse this non-observance.

—Niccolò Machiavelli, *The Prince*

"[To] defeat a revolution, you must become the revolution."

—Corey Robin, *The Reactionary Mind*

On Constitutional Reform

March 12, 2011

Revolutions are tumultuous. This is the first article in a series that will tackle the tumult by discussing the obstacles standing in the way of the full realization of the revolution's goals. The series title should not be seen as a dismissal of the colossal accomplishments of the revolution but rather a desire to see them enshrined and sustained in the new republic of Egypt.

Throughout the eighteen days of protests that started on January 25, Egyptians demanded the "fall of the regime." And while February 11 was celebrated like any major feat, most realize that the end of a regime is not simply the fall of its patriarch, but rather the dismantling of the structure that anchored him. For this reason, one of the earliest demands of the revolutionaries was the amendment of the constitution to guarantee Egyptians equal opportunities for political participation. Many months before the revolution, the National Association for Change (NAC) initiated a campaign to collect one million signatures demanding constitutional amendments that would reverse the numerous prohibitive clauses that made democracy impossible and concentrated power in the hands of the formerly ruling National Democratic Party (NDP).

Shortly after President Hosni Mubarak's resignation, in a step to address the revolution's demands, the Supreme Council of the Armed Forces (SCAF) appointed a committee led by Chancellor Tariq al-Bishri to review the constitution and draft amendments to open up parliamentary and presidential election processes. From the outset, the committee was criticized for failing to represent the majority of Egyptian society. For example, Nawal El Saadawy offered a scathing condemnation of the committee for failing to include women, and many Copts complained that it did not consult Coptic legislators. Nevertheless, most waited to see what the committee would propose.

Admittedly, some of the proposed amendments resonated with public demands. For instance: article 77 limits the president's service to two terms, each lasting four years; article 88 reestablishes complete judicial oversight of the electoral process; article 139 requires the appointment of a vice president; article 148 permits the extension of a state of emergency beyond a six-month period only by public referendum; and article 93 gives the Supreme Constitutional Court the authority to decide on the validity of membership in the People's Assembly. Tamir Moustafa, the author of *The Struggle for Constitutional Power: Law, Politics, and Economic Development in Egypt* (2007) and a professor at Simon Fraser University, has expressed some optimism about the amendments, saying that while they "do not constitute a fundamental break from the past, they do open a viable path to further political reform."

However, most analysts and constitutional experts have argued that the amendments are insufficient because they are grafted onto a defunct and corrupt constitution that needs extensive revision. At a recent briefing in Washington, D.C. organized by the Arab-American Anti-Discrimination Committee (ADC), Sahar Aziz, adjunct professor of law at Georgetown University, discussed the loopholes in the constitution. She argued that "limited constitutional reforms cannot replace the necessary comprehensive legal reforms required to transition to an effective and sustainable democracy." She further suggested that "the pace of reform should slow down to permit new parties, especially those that will represent the youth and minority groups, to develop and competitively run for parliamentary offices."

Many believe the amendments to article 76—regarding the eligibility for presidential nomination—are still too restrictive. It suggests that the candidate must be endorsed by thirty members of the People's Assembly or the Shura Council, collect thirty thousand signatures from Egyptians from fifteen governorates, or be a member of a party that holds at least one seat in parliament. Given the current political parties in Egypt, their underrepresentation in the last parliament, and weak public outreach due to decades of marginalization, these conditions are prohibitive. Article 76 is far more problematic for subsequent elections, as nomination will require securing sixty-five members of the People's Assembly, twenty-five members of the Shura Council, and ten members of local councils in at least fourteen governorates. This is a near-impossible feat for a candidate without significant means and strong institutional support, and may therefore privilege former regime members. Article 76 needs to be completely rewritten to create a more accessible road to the presidency for more eligible Egyptians.

Aziz further argues that the Emergency Law needs to be amended to limit the use of military courts in adjudicating criminal matters. Political party laws need urgent revision to ensure functional and viable political participation, as do the laws governing the registration and legal parameters of nongovernmental organizations (NGOs) and civil society institutions. For these and many other reasons, few of the revolutionary groups have expressed any real optimism about the amendments suggested.

Mohamed ElBaradei rejected the amendments outright and called for a complete review of the document. This would require more time and force a reversal of the election schedule outlined by the Supreme Council of the Armed Forces—constitutional referendum, parliamentary elections, and finally presidential elections. ElBaradei has pressed for a "presidential council" to oversee government affairs and supervise this process, which would serve until a conducive timeline for changes is instituted. A conference entitled "Dustur Baladna" (Our Country's Constitution) was held on March 7 to discuss the proposed amendments. The resolutions announced by the participants reiterated ElBaradei's call that the 1971 constitution be annulled completely.

Lest anyone forget, the last time the constitution was amended, in 2007, the modifications of thirty-four articles passed in a sham referendum marred with irregularities and minuscule voter participation. Despite the NDP's iron grip on the process and a predetermined outcome, the greatest problem for the amendment's opponents still prevails today—the majority of Egyptians are not acquainted with the constitution at all. Even of those who have some awareness of it, many might be tempted to accept the draft by the rosy language of the amendments or because they feel enough has been accomplished already.

While the revolutionaries did call for quick action, they did not ask to forgo either the people's right to negotiate the constitutional changes or sufficient time to inform the public about the repercussions of the proposed amendments if passed. By setting the referendum date as March 19, it appears the military's rush to confirm the amendments will come at the expense of informed public participation. And unless revolutionary groups can rally swiftly and effectively against the amendments, they run the risk of seeing them pass and losing a genuine opportunity for change.

To get their way, the revolutionaries must convince the Supreme Council of the Armed Forces and prime minister Essam Sharaf's government to scrap the referendum altogether and resort to another approach. This has already begun with full-fledged campaigns in the print media, on television, and online. With barely a week before the scheduled vote, the armed forces have set up a committee to monitor reactions to the proposals. A branch of the cabinet also created a poll page to survey public opinion. So far the majority of votes are opposed. However, there is no guarantee that the military will comply. So far, they appear intent on moving forward with the March 19 vote.

If the referendum does proceed, those in power now will likely benefit from the dilemma that stands before Egyptians at the voting stations — take what is being offered and postpone substantial change, or opt for the most ambitious but uncertain outcome. And while a revolution by definition is a complete overhaul and not a concession to the old state of affairs, many Egyptians are increasingly wary of further dissent. Those who want to see the revolution fully realized must do the impossible. In record time, they must convince the majority of Egyptians of the counterintuitive: that the only road to real reform is to say 'no' to what looks like real reform. But this revolution has repeatedly shown it is capable of the impossible.

Liberating the Media

April 1, 2011

On June 7, 1967, Egyptians nationwide sat glued to their radio sets listening to the news bulletin about a war involving many of their beloved sons. While most were anxious and worried, there was an air of optimism. As a patriotic song came to an end, the familiar and trusted voice of announcer Ahmad Said came on air. In his characteristically confident tone he announced, "The glorious and blessed Egyptian Air Force has forced defeat on its enemy. In the early hours of the morning, four enemy fighter aircraft were shot down and eight tanks destroyed. Our nation's army has also made significant advances and captured hundreds of enemy prisoners." The faces of those huddled around the radio turned from frowns to smiles. They applauded, rejoiced, held hands, and hugged one another repeatedly.

It was only a couple of days before they learned that Ahmad Said's news report was completely fictitious. Instead all the reports were concocted to deflect attention from the catastrophic losses Egypt and its Arab allies were facing at the hands of the Israeli military. The Six Day War didn't simply lead to Egypt's loss of the Sinai Peninsula (6 percent of the country's land mass), the death of ten thousand to fifteen thousand troops, and the annihilation of its air force, it also laid to rest the Arab world's then most powerful revolutionary broadcasters—Voice of the Arabs. Its iconic and beloved demagogue, Ahmad Said, lost all legitimacy and credibility in the wake of the barrage of fabrications he uttered for six days. In fact, so convincing was Said that when the news came out that Egypt had been bitterly defeated, most Egyptians were in a state of complete shock, disbelief, and denial.

Since then and for the last forty-five years, Egyptian television has been stunted. Bland, dull, unimaginative, and chronically incapable of delivering accurate and relevant news in an appealing fashion, state television has been on autopilot and content with simply existing. And while Egypt was the first Arab country to export its product regionally over satellite, the Egyptian Satellite Channel resigned itself to the B-list of satellite stations. It was only nudged into a stylistic facelift in the mid-2000s with the advent of high-budget Gulf-based channels like Al Jazeera and the private Egyptian channels like Dream, Mehwar, ONTV, and others. It nevertheless continued unabated in its excessively airbrushed presentation of Egypt's deteriorating economic and political situation.

However, with the revolution in full force, few thought the state's toothless and incompetent television would actually revert to Voice of the Arabs strategies of completely fraudulent reports of the protests. In retrospect, the content from those eighteen days has since become iconic—from fake foreign-trained protesters and KFC conspiracies to an empty Tahrir Square and massive pro-Mubarak rallies. State television's calamitous fall from grace effectively turned Maspero into another Tahrir where protesters gathered to challenge coverage.

These blunders allowed some of the Egyptian private stations to come of age during the revolution. Most of them held entertainment and specialty licenses, and most adopted the late-night, prime-time talk format and became exceptionally popular as audiences were transfixed by competing interviews with notable figures, revolutionaries, and politicians (hosted by television presenters Mona El Shazly, Yosri Fouda, Reem Maged, Wael al-Ibrashi, and the like). Some carried iconic interviews that shifted public opinion considerably during and following the revolution, such as Wael Ghoneim's captivating interview with Mona El Shazly following his release from prison. These stations would steal the limelight and make television history with shows like the ONTV sparring match between prime minister Ahmad Shafiq and writer Alaa Al Aswany, which some have credited for the resignation of Shafiq's government. Nowadays, few nights aren't accented with captivating programs featuring Amr Moussa, Mohamed ElBaradei, Naguib Sawiris, Amr Hamzawi, Sadat assassination plotter Abbud al-Zumur, Salafi cleric Shaykh Muhammad Hassan, and others. All of this has happened while Egyptian state television has largely sat idly by—either in an attempt to derail the revolution or simply perplexed about how to manage the inevitable.

The only thing that stands in the way of progress in Egyptian media is the stubbornly slow pace of institutional reform. For over a month,

al-Ahram's deputy editor Sabah Hamamou and colleagues have staged protests to persuade prime minister Essam Sharaf's caretaker government to
dispose of Mubarakite editor in chief Usama Saraya. The decision finally
came on March 30, as all the editors of all the state-owned newspapers
were replaced. Sharaf is promising the same will happen at Maspero.

Despite the positive gestures, I remain unconvinced that anything
less than a complete overhaul of Egypt's media system will produce lasting results. The first step must be a courageous and drastic one—the
complete dismantling of the Ministry of Information and its relegation
to the annals of Egyptian authoritarian history. What would remain in
its place is an institution responsible for regulating media and communications in the country with strict and narrowly defined parameters to
do so—from issuing licenses to prohibiting government and corporate
media monopoly. The Egyptian Radio and Television Union should either
take on these responsibilities or live up to its name and become a union to
represent the interests of the two sectors' employees. It should also limit
its intervention in regional and transnational broadcasting by refraining
from disruption of operations on Nilesat, which had become a customary
occurrence during the Mubarak era.

Furthermore, the infamous State Information Service (SIS), the
country's ugly external face, should also be fully defrocked. It has been
a conglomeration of the most propagandistic elements of the ministries
of Information and Foreign Affairs, state security, and the intelligence
services. For decades, the SIS has undermined any transparent or critical
view of the Egyptian state in the eyes of the world. Their website declares
that the National Democratic Party was the first party in Egypt and was
founded in 1907 by Mustafa Kamil! And while the site describes Mubarak
as ex-president, it still counts the present day under the "Mubarak era
(1981–)"! But this is neither a mistake nor irony. We are in fact still in the
Mubarak era. The old regime may not exist in the Egyptian street or in the
offices of government, but it dwells deep in the bellies of the bureaucracy
that owes its very existence to him.

The institution that manufactures underqualified journalists who
are trained to be subservient to authority remains steadfast in its paternalistic ways. Sami Abd al-Aziz, the dean of Cairo University's College
of Mass Communication, a high-ranking NDP official and friend of the
Mubaraks, has been at the center of a firestorm demonstration by students who were striking and starving themselves to force him out of his

office. He withstood this bout of activism with the assistance of a violent intervention by the armed forces, who beat and Tasered students. This is the stubbornness of the Mubarakites.

On and off Cairo University's campus, the Supreme Council of the Armed Forces is the new executive branch. They pose the greatest challenge to Egypt's newfound media freedom with their violations ignored, dismissed, overlooked, or suppressed. A disturbing example is a recent episode of ONTV's show with Yosri Fouda, which featured a call from an unnamed high-ranking member of the military. Besides his clearly discouraging tone, his anonymity spoke volumes about the possibility of an ominous future for Egyptian media. The invisibility of the armed forces flies in the face of free media. Talk-show hosts treat military officials with reverence. Even when criticism of their conduct is warranted, questions are posed as if accusations are unfounded suspicions. The top brass are invited to dispel these and anchors react with satisfaction and affirmation.

In a post-Mubarak era, state radio and television should be responsible to the public. They should be under the supervision and scrutiny of citizens, not under the paternalistic guidance of state bureaucrats or the military establishment. Now is the time to end the media's blind pursuit of popular consensus with the farcical excuse of protecting national security and maintaining stability.

The Ax-bearers

May 16, 2011

T he night's events in the neighborhood of Imbaba began with a Salafi flash-mob demonstration in front of the St. Mina church demanding the release of a Coptic woman convert to Islam. Christian and Muslim youths converged on the church to defend it against a possible attack. As the fires grew in the courtyard of the church, the voices of crowds reverberated into the night sky, "Muslim, Christian, one hand." At the end of the night, the streets around the church had been turned into battlefields, blood had been spilled, and the smell of smoldering ash rose into the air. Fingers of blame were pointing in every direction.

Christians accused Salafis and *baltagiya* (thugs). Salafis accused Christians and *baltagiya*. The Supreme Council of the Armed Forces condemned the *baltagiya*. The government said it would take decisive action against Muslim and Christian *baltagiya*. In a span of twenty-four hours everyone in Egypt was a likely *baltagi*, from the urban poor to the Coptic pope Shenouda. But the real question is: Whom did the *baltagiya* accuse? So I went on a quest to locate a *baltagi* to get his opinion. Sadly, I learned that the *baltagiya* have no office, no phone number, no representatives, no websites, no e-mail addresses, no Facebook profiles or Twitter feeds (spoofs aside). No one has come forward to admit being a member of this elite force of divisiveness. So there is no one to speak for the *baltagiya*. This is because they have no names, faces, or leaders. So who are these invisible *baltagiya* that seem to pose such a major threat to the contiguity of the Egyptian revolution? Arguably, they are now the most influential group in post-Mubarak Egypt.

They are part of the storyline in every act of violence in Egypt since the revolution. They were accused of the attacks on the churches in Atfih and Imbaba, and the clashes in al-Zabbalin two months ago. They are condemned publicly as the perpetrators of attacks against public figures, such as the one that prevented reform advocate Mohamed ElBaradei from voting during the constitutional amendments. While they are often described as a professional class of violent thugs, the *baltagiya* likely come in two or more varieties. Some are institutionalized into the state security apparatus, making them indistinguishable from the surveillance force of the plainclothes police. Others are fearless, time- and battle-tested freelance operators who can act as an unofficial urban mercenary force. The former are an unconventional instrument of law enforcement who are immune from scrutiny, the latter a loose force that can provide its services to the highest bidder and shoulder all the public disdain.

Even before the revolution, the *baltagiya* were a mainstay in Egyptian cinema and television, where they exist and function outside the law. They are often depicted as part of a parallel legal system—a missing link between elite hegemons and the unruly masses. As in reality, they did the dirty work of the police and the powerful. In a stable police state, the *baltagiya* are known entities, individuals to be feared and revered. But in post–February 11 Egypt, they have become anonymous, the masked actors on behalf of what the government, military, media, and public now call generically the "hidden hands." While they may eventually be arrested, tried, and sentenced for crimes, they are insulated by layers of misdirection, making their sponsors practically untraceable.

The only thing more serious than what the so-called *baltagiya* do is what they represent. One cannot understand their impact without understanding the discourse behind their representation. The word *baltagi* in Arabic means 'he who bears an ax,' with the old Turkish suffix modification still common in many parts of the Arab world. It has been used for decades in the Egyptian vernacular, with negative connotations implying hired thugs and members of violent urban gangs. Today it has become what linguists call a 'floating signifier,' a word that doesn't point to any actual or agreed-upon meaning. The term itself carries no other identity, since it does not communicate any sociological, political, cultural, economic, ideological, or religious meaning. The only common usage for the term suggests absolute opportunism outside of any basic humanitarian principles, values, or ethics. Yet it is precisely this absence of a denotative meaning that makes the term most dangerous.

And incidentally, the confusion in its meaning coincides with the increase in its use. Out of curiosity, I did a quick search of the word *baltagiya* in the Arabic press over the last few years. While this is by no means an accurate content or discourse analysis, it is nevertheless telling about the usage of the term. In 2008, the word *baltagiya* was used in a total of 105 articles. In the following year, the number increased to 196. It was not until 2010 that *baltagiya* came into regular usage, when it featured in 896 articles, the majority of these published in November and December during and after the parliamentary elections. The term was used to describe the regime's intimidation of the public and opposition candidates during this period. However, 2011 has proven to be the year of *baltagiya*, as the term appeared in 3,809 articles between January and May, a fourfold increase in just a few months. What September 11 did for the term 'terrorists,' the Egyptian revolution did for the word *baltagiya*.

During the eighteen days of protests that toppled Mubarak, the term that was a weapon in the hands of the regime's opponents was being hijacked by the government to characterize the protesters. The sheer negativity of the term in colloquial Egyptian made it a useful instrument to discredit the 'other.' Since February 11, with the term still devoid of actual meaning, it has become legalized. The new authority in Egypt today and the only institution above the law, the Supreme Council of the Armed Forces, has appropriated it to accuse and sentence anyone it sees fit. Extrajudicial military court sentences have been handed down for blogging, public expressions, and calls to demonstrate and strike. Today, the newly activated "Law of Baltaga" (thuggery) can be used in a manner akin to the Emergency Law and the penal code against anyone who might be perceived as a threat to the security of the state, extending even to cases of so-called 'online *baltaga*.'

The move to install a legal condition for an undefined category was swift, forgetting what precipitated it. *Baltagiya* are actually victims of the Mubarak system. They are a product of the failing neoliberal economic project and its polarization of the rich and poor. They are those who were forced into a life of commissioned crime by the disappearance of the middle class and the state's need to maintain order despite the drastic disequilibrium. Furthermore, the NDP had effectively institutionalized them to facilitate the conditions necessary for its consolidation of power—from intimidation of opposition election candidates to maintaining conformity in Cairo's combustible and underprivileged slums, to protecting the physical assets of the powerful and wealthy, to instilling a general state of fear. Take the infamous "Battle of the Camel" of February

2–3, 2011, where poor, desperate, and misinformed camel and horse riders were transformed into *baltagiya* with food, money, and the instructions to attack what they were told was a demonstration responsible for the tourism slump that cost them their livelihoods. This goes to the core of the *baltagiya* phenomenon. Rather than being seen as natural-born criminals whose intent and conviction is for violence, they must be viewed as tools, not perpetrators, the product of a socioeconomic catastrophe.

The true *baltagiya* are those who will not and cannot be tried using the Law of Baltaga, but rather will be protected by it, as the toughened underprivileged pragmatists they hire take the blame and the country pays the price. In Egypt today, no evidence is necessary to render a protester or a petty thief a *baltagi*, but those who profit in the billions from illegal business dealings must undergo elaborate, inconclusive investigations. Sadly, an untraceable pact seems to have emerged between those too desperate to operate legally and those who desperately use the law to operate illegally. What is at stake in this alliance is no less than the future of Egypt if the latter are not stopped.

The greatest danger posed by *baltagiya* is not that they instill a state of uncertainty, fear, and paranoia in the country, or that they create a culture of violence, or that they foment divisions among the revolutionaries (such as the recent sectarianism), or that they distract from the revolution's priorities, or that they might be ushering in, through their actions, a virulent form of military totalitarianism in Egypt. Instead, the *baltagiya* are most frightening because their very existence, at least as a rhetorical and legal construction, creates a space above the law. Beyond simply serving as a scapegoat that can be easily demonized, vilified, and eventually punished, they are a shroud that conceals the real actors who sponsor unrest in the country. With the sentencing of every so-called *baltagi*, a funder and endorser of instability in Egypt escapes justice. As the witch hunt unfolds against the *baltagiya*, those intent on assassinating the revolution remain at large.

Revolutionary Fatigues

June 10, 2011

It is one thing for a revolution to face off against a regime or counterrevolutionary forces; it is another thing when it has to confront another revolution. January 25 was supposed to be the ultimate supreme revolution among revolutions in Egyptian history. But that wasn't the plan the ruling military council had in mind. While commemorating the protests and harping on about having protecting the protesters or being biased in their favor, the military has had to ensure that the memory of its very own revolution of July 26, 1952 is not forgotten. Unlike 1952, which the armed forces can make a somewhat convincing argument to have instigated, 2011 is a popular uprising where the military was a latecomer.

It is for this reason that in the year 2011, SCAF has spent much of its time overstating its historic accomplishments, commemorating its victories, and congratulating itself for its wise administration of the country, while simultaneously vilifying the revolutionaries and dismissing them from the political arena that they engineer. Instead, it is the Muslim Brotherhood, SCAF's "friends with benefits," who have been compliant in the first eight months since the toppling of Mubarak. They have said everything right and stand to benefit and gain when the elections come around, as SCAF engineers parliamentary elections that will privilege established parties over unaffiliated individuals or independents. The Brotherhood and SCAF seem to share a central nervous system these days, to the detriment of the revolution. Their most dangerous act is the repetition of a purely fictitious line of judgment: "The military protected the revolution." Not only did the military watch like a spectator at a tennis match as Molotovs and all kinds of ammunition were fired on Tahrir during the eighteen days, they also oversaw a violent breakup of a Tahrir sit-in on March 9, less than a month after Mubarak's toppling, during which detainees were beaten and tortured and convincing reports of young women subjected to virginity tests were offered.

Perhaps SCAF was protecting the revolution when it released bulletins accusing the April 6 Youth Movement and various youth leaders of being foreign-funded, disloyal traitors, after SCAF celebrated a revolution whose protests they played a role in triggering. Essentially the military has learned from the mistakes of other security apparatuses. While the NDP, police authorities, and other institutions always showed *al-ayn al-zarqa* (the blue eye)—meaning severe punishment such as unapologetic stubborn condescension toward the public—SCAF has turned to another approach altogether. Rather than choosing between the stick and the carrot, it is deploying both simultaneously while sugarcoating everything with gentle benevolent embraces that suggest companionship. They address the people of Egypt as if endorsing the revolution, its values, and its demands wholeheartedly, in some instances even memorializing its martyrs, rendering them heroes in the eyes of the state. But how has the army dealt with these protesters?

The army attacked the monastery of St. Bishoy in the desert of Wadi al-Natrun, Using live rounds, firing at the monastery's sign, it used tanks to knock down the surrounding fence and one of the entrances, accompanied by over a hundred soldiers. At the least, this was disproportionate, and at the most, it was inappropriate, violent, and offensive. Elsewhere, new law enforcement officers are being trained to see fellow Egyptians as animals, or as humans of a lesser breed. The head of administrative security in Bahariya was caught in a uncensored and candid conversation with high-ranking members of his law enforcement team. He said that anyone breaking the law would be punished, and he appeared to egg them on to be merciless with protesters, saying that if they resist, "then you can beat them with your shoes; you are their masters." And while the military has escaped scrutiny throughout the last thirty years, with few daring to ask any questions about it, today they are front and center. Their presence in the spotlight following a people's revolution will certainly challenge their ability to dictate. However, it is too early for the public to scrutinize them. Their Facebook page has over 500,000 likes and has become one of the main ways for them to communicate. This is a far cry from their starting point.

A couple of years ago, in my conversations with several editors in chief of independent newspapers, I inquired whether there was an absolute red line in their coverage, beyond self-censorship and the fear of the government panopticon. Across the board, all of them said it was the military. Notoriously camera-shy, the military began giving interviews just prior to the revolution so as to familiarize some journalists with its nationalistic role in safeguarding the country. One wonders what the rationale is behind this. Yet the military's most powerful weapon to win Egyptians' hearts and minds (apologies for the ultra-American realpolitik cliché), was actually Libyan dictator Muammar Qadhafi. SCAF had craftily avoided scrutiny, especially in comparison to the atrocities committed by Qadhafi's military and special forces against protesters. Watching this on their television screens, Egyptians were made to feel relieved that at least their own military did not use force against them.

Their other tactic to abort the revolution has been to divide and conquer among the protesters. Some of the latter have been very critical of the military from the outset, but most are reluctant to get on their bad side. There is continued concern that if the protesters lose the military, then they have nothing else on their side. Conversely, the military is trying not to lose the public and risk facing a full-fledged public mutiny. Instead they are banking on a growing disinterest in protests and revolution fatigue. Yet this is the primal fear of the revolutionaries—that their revolution has hit a fortified wall. All evidence seems to suggest that SCAF has in fact built this wall, both figuratively and literally.

In the end, SCAF's argument is that the revolution succeeded and was concluded on February 11. They have dressed the January 25 Revolution in military fatigues and punished anyone who resists. What they haven't realized is that if they try to swallow the revolution, they will choke on it.

Who's Your Daddy?

July 25, 2011

I am torn between two fathers. Both are from the same generation, both have roots in Upper Egypt, and both are the embodiment of fatherhood. One is a shared public father for everyone, and the other is a personal father. My public father is a leader who is often spoken of in the home, street, and school. He is everywhere, like nature. Like the water, air, soil, or rays of the sun. My personal private dad is different. In a moment, I can run into his bedroom."

Nine-year-old Nada Abd al-Qadir narrates a reality for generations of Egyptians. She is the embattled protagonist in Radwa Ashour's 2008 novel *Farag* whose Sorbonne-educated father was imprisoned by her "public father" Gamal Abd al-Nasser in 1959 for espousing "questionable" views. The absence of her biological father and the omnipresence of the nation's caregiver confused Nada. Despite her pride in her father, she says "it was Nasser who raised me." Later in life, Nada would herself join a line of family members who were imprisoned for their political dissidence at the hands of Egypt's successive totalitarian "fathers."

For millennia, Egypt's "fathers" have been omnipresent. They adorned every public space in the country, from sphinxes in their likeness and obelisks describing their insurmountable achievements, to every government office and street corner decorated with varnished, doctored photos of their younger selves. Since his assumption of the presidency, Hosni Mubarak has tried to craft a different kind of image for himself compared to his predecessors. In contrast to Nasser's image as the consummate populist leader and Sadat's wily, wiser-than-thou, visionary depiction, Mubarak adopted the image of a benevolent, tolerant, and compassionate father. Of the three, his was the only officially commissioned photograph where the president smiled, as if comfortingly saying, "With me, everything is all right." While his characteristic smile led some to dub him *"la vache qui rit"* (the laughing cow, after a brand of French cheese), it deceptively concealed Egypt's slow and crippling deterioration. This was a father whose inability to judge the severity of his country's ailments was beyond even the parody of leadership in Albert Cossery's novel *The Joker*.

Egyptian fathers are expected to provide. In his thirty-year paternal tenure, Mubarak transformed a caregiver state into one that punished its people. He spoke of bounty but provided none of it. He expressed egalitarianism but acted preferentially. He advocated for the masses but empowered the few. He claimed to be building a meritocracy but made nepotism the status quo. And he did it all while smiling at Egyptians everywhere they looked. For most, he was a wolf in sheep's clothing, a father whose kind exterior hid his ruthless core. And to some, Mubarak was the blemish-free and kind father without whose watchful eye we could not function or survive. Those were the blindly obedient who advocated for so-called stability and security throughout the eighteen days of protest, whom Egyptians have mockingly called the "Couch Party."

After Mubarak's seemingly permanent move to Sharm al-Sheikh after February 11, the Couch Party developed new approaches to old agendas—celebrate the revolution, appropriate its symbols and accomplishments, demand an end to demands, and attack the protesters, figuratively and literally. Today members of the Couch Party have descended onto the streets in their meager hundreds, labeling themselves the "silent majority," to disempower the unfinished revolution. Buoyed by a court decision to overturn a ruling to remove the name and image of Mubarak and his family from public establishments, they converged on Roxy Square to apologize, to honor him, and to plead for continued military rule. With the encouragement of Supreme Council of the Armed Forces' smear campaign to demonize the April 6 Youth Movement, the silent majority turned into a violent minority, attacking peaceful protesters marching toward the Ministry of Defense headquarters. All the while, Egypt's new foster father, SCAF, has condoned 'public' actions against its critics, with central security and military police providing cover.

The latest episode involves a smear campaign by SCAF member General Hasan al-Ruwayni, who accused the April 6 Youth Movement of receiving foreign assistance in the form of training in peaceful protest at the hands of the Serbian student movement Otpor! The irony of this claim is deplorable and laughable in equal measure. It should be no secret to anyone that the military is the country's largest single recipient of foreign assistance, with $1.3 billion annually from the U.S. government alone. Clearly, they are turning to the age-old fathers' mantra, "Do as I say, not as I do."

But the military's camouflage uniforms have started to wear off. For a revolution that takes pride in its leaderlessness, the army's only option has been to try and remain outside the limelight, concealing their role as the political puppeteers in the barely post-Mubarak era. Yet there is no mistake; SCAF is calling all the shots behind closed doors, engineering their invisible yet endless presence in Egyptian political and economic life while carefully deflecting attention and scrutiny. Signs of this are now aplenty, but it is hardly more evident than in an incident relayed by Hossam Bahgat, of the Egyptian Initiative for Personal Rights (EIPR), who attended a British embassy reception with 150 other invitees on June 9 to commemorate the queen's birthday. The newly appointed U.K. ambassador James Watt dutifully stood up and raised a toast in honor of Field Marshal Tantawi, referring to him as "Egypt's acting president." Evidently, in the hallways of power, there is no people's revolution. What does this mean? Could this revolution be a remarkable and historic sleight of hand? Has SCAF packaged and delivered a soft coup d'état in a civilian revolution's gift-wrapping?

In this ongoing struggle between competing powers—street versus state apparatus—Egypt's authorities may have miscalculated and underestimated the revolutionaries' threshold for infantilization. This is not the same country where the child Nada Abd al-Qadir revered her "public father," Nasser. Instead, she has now come of age, dissented, and disowned all forms of patriarchy. Egypt's interim rulers must realize their rule is necessarily interim. The new Egypt no longer bows to paternalism, but rather rejoices in its orphanhood.

After Maspero

October 15, 2011

The megaphone was passed to her not because she was a leader or a seasoned chanter. Sure, she was a recurring face at many of the Tahrir protests, but Heba was far from being an organizer. She was given the megaphone because all the other sloganeers had lost their voices in the last two hours of shouting as they marched out of al-Azhar Mosque toward Tahrir Square—the epicenter of the Egyptian revolution. Heba tightened her veil by tugging on the fabric until it reached her hairline, folded the corners in front of her ears, and brought the megaphone up to her mouth. She took a deep breath, and with fresh vocal cords she let out a screeching cry: "*Yasqut, yasqut hukm al-'askar!*" (Down, down with military rule!).

I had been advised not to venture out that day, but I hadn't listened. Protests were now deemed extremely dangerous and everyone knew that in a moment's time things could get ugly. Just a few days prior, I was sitting in front of the television transfixed by live coverage of a tragedy unfolding. Thirty-one protesters had been killed at a rally. It seemed the powers that be were trying to scare us out of civil disobedience. For the few days that followed, the scare tactic worked. Enraged and confused, I stayed home, as did most activists. But the agony of solitary commiseration was unbearable. I needed to know I wasn't alone in my mourning, my anger, and my outrage. So, on the first Friday after the attack, and without informing anyone, I left the house and made my way through the surprisingly quiet roads of downtown Cairo to the one place that every Egyptian can call home—Tahrir Square.

I am not certain what I was looking for or expecting. But upon arrival, I found nothing. Tahrir was unusually empty. Very few vendors or carts were around. Business was nonexistent and visitors to the iconic square had dwindled to none. A visceral feeling of melancholy came over me. It was just eight months ago when Egyptians overcame fear, protested in the millions in this very square, and toppled their stubborn autocrat. But today, in the face of another tragedy, it was barren and lifeless. In my head, I cursed those who had once again instilled fear in the hearts of Egyptians once again. As if to console myself, I convinced myself that while most Egyptians were in their homes and chose not to take to the streets to mourn their fallen brethren, they were all unanimously supportive of their cause. They all lived in a virtual Tahrir. They all sympathized with the families of the martyrs. But there was no evidence of this. I could not prove my hopes.

I wandered around looking for anyone to speak to, any conversation to seek consolation from. I found a group of five men standing next to a sidewalk littered with the day's newspapers. They were discussing "the incident," in a very quiet tone, making my attempt at eavesdropping extremely difficult. It was a sensitive time. Everyone was fearful and paranoid. One of the men saw me. He inched closer to his friends and alerted them to my presence. "Even the walls have ears," he said while giving me a suspicious stare. They fell silent, moved a few meters away, and huddled closer. Since when did people in Tahrir watch over their shoulders and censor themselves? This square, the birthplace of Egyptian freedom, had been overtaken by fear and paranoia. The extreme violence of "the incident" left the revolutionaries weary, fearful, disenchanted, psychologically scarred, and reluctant to continue demonstrating. This wasn't the home of bustling democratic expression, where every Egyptian came to speak his mind. It seemed the revolution had come to an end. An eerie silence hung over Tahrir. I sat down on the edge of the sidewalk and stared at the empty square with a somber lament.

"*Yasqut, yasqut hukm al-'askar!*"

"Down, down with military rule!"

The sound of fury tore through the silence. Heba's voice on the megaphone erupted from the farthest end of the square, "*Yasqut, yasqut hukm al-'askar!*"

I leapt to my feet and cautiously approached the source of the sound. As if breathing new life into the square, the chants brought people out from neighboring streets to get a closer look. As the march approached Tahrir Square, Heba's voice grew louder and more urgent, "The people demand the fall of the field marshal!"

"Yasqut, yasqut hukm al-'askar!"
"Yasqut, yasqut hukm al-'askar!"
A feeling of relief and contentment came upon me as I heard the voices of the protesters reverberate in the afternoon air. The revolution had not succumbed.

Heba had come out on this afternoon to register her fury at the violence, the injustice, and the incitement. The chant against the military had become standardized in the months that followed the fall of the Mubarak government, as the ruling Supreme Council of the Armed Forces (SCAF) slowly demoralized the youth revolutionaries, committed atrocities against them, and locked them out of political deal-making. But this chant had a particular resonance that day after "the incident." Just a few days ago, on October 9, 2011, and only a couple of kilometers away from Tahrir, the blood of Coptic (Egyptian Orthodox Christian) protesters was spilled at the doorstep of Maspero, the infamous Egyptian state radio and television building.

The October 9 marchers had come out en masse to challenge the military's conduct of the post-Mubarak transition period. There had been an unusual spike in sectarian violence against Copts and their places of worship. While all Christians around the country were pained by the uncharacteristic violence, most found the incidents to be suspicious. In just eight months, Egypt had witnessed more attacks against Christians than in any period in recent memory, and virtually all of these seemed unprovoked and not in line with popular public sentiments. They felt someone was trying to sow the seeds of hatred between Egyptians. As the months went on, with no one brought to justice on any of these counts, and with the ruling military junta doing little to resolve suspicion, Copts began turning their frustration toward SCAF. They had failed to protect or secure Christian communities and did little to assuage their fears. So when a church was attacked in Aswan and the governor of the southern governorate claimed the building was not a licensed place of worship, Christian protesters and Muslim sympathizers staged a march to Maspero. Many of those marching in this procession had begun pointing fingers not at their Muslim brethren but at SCAF, which they believed was benefiting from a climate of sectarian tension that would derail the revolution.

"Yasqut, yasqut hukm al-'askar!" "Down, down with military rule!" shouted the unusually courageous crowd who paraded out of the densely populated

and cosmopolitan area of Shubra (within walking distance of downtown Cairo) holding candles and carrying crosses. Many had come out with their families. Mothers and fathers brought their children to exercise a right never accorded to them during the Mubarak era. Empowered by a new Egypt and propelled by calls for justice, they demanded that the military step down in the face of a wave of sectarian violence that SCAF were at best unable to deal with, and at worst were implicitly stoking. But it seemed the military was in no mood to be challenged. Minutes later, these protesters would be brutally attacked by those charged with protecting them.

The perpetrators of the attack, unimaginably, were Egypt's own military. In an absurdly ironic David-versus-Goliath scenario, the state's most powerful institution and the country's weakest minority had collided, leaving thirty-one Christian demonstrators dead and hundreds injured. Many of those killed had either been mowed down by armored vehicles or shot by live ammunition.

As the sounds of screams and wails tore through the nighttime sky, in a studio whose windows looks onto the carnage a news anchor powdered her nose before the "On Air" light came on. And when it flashed, she was in tens of millions of Egyptian homes simultaneously, informing them of what was happening outside her building. When she opened her mouth, she declared: "Violent Coptic protesters attacked the military, killing three soldiers and injuring many!" It did not stop there. She called on the "honorable people of Egypt" to come out and defend their armed forces. Very few answered the call. But those who did went on a witch hunt looking for Christians who, they were led to believe, had perpetrated crimes against Egypt's heroes in uniform. Mobs armed with swords, knives, clubs, and makeshift weapons wandered around Maspero inspecting everyone's wrists for tattoos of crosses, which are common markings among Copts. During the eighteen days of protests that toppled Mubarak, Christians stood hand-in-hand around their Muslim brethren to protect them during their prayers from the attacks of pro-Mubarak mobs. They would raise their hands to reveal their cross tattoos as a sign of interfaith solidarity. But on October 9, these same tattoos turned into targets of reprisal. Egypt after Mubarak, it seemed, had descended to a new low.

The incident was so disturbing it paralyzed Egyptians. People sat in their homes, watching conflicting coverage of the events. State television absolved the military and accused the predominantly Christian protesters. Some private networks showed the reality of the horror, going to coverage from the morgues and hospitals where bodies were strewn across the floor. Many had been mutilated, contorted, and flattened beyond recognition under the weight of armored vehicles. At no point in the Mubarak era had anything this vile and grotesque occurred, not even when the regime was in its final throes and down to its last breath. The delicate balance of Egypt's religious diversity had been disrupted. No one knew what this meant and what could be done to rectify the situation. The whole country seemed to have frozen in time.

But not for Heba. With the trauma of that day still fresh and palpable, her eyes scanned Tahrir. There were more onlookers in the square than participants, and only a handful echoed her chants. People still seemed puzzled, unsure, and afraid. Who had committed crimes against whom? Who was the victim and who was the perpetrator? Should they believe Heba's criticism of the military or the state television anchor from a few days ago? Heba was getting infuriated by the blank stares all around her. "How could they not be outraged?" she thought to herself. Her voice cracked. She was overcome with misery and sorrow. It was then that she broke from the typical chants and improvised an off-key slogan, "*Al-aqbaat ash'ab adeya!*" (The Copts have a righteous cause!) At a time when everyone seemed a fence-sitter, Heba took a side. The small protesting crowd that came with her repeated:

"*Al-aqbaat ash'ab adeya!*"

"The Copts have a righteous cause!"

The couple of hundred protesters marched around Tahrir in hope of picking up more supporters and veered onto a side street en route to the cathedral in Abbasiya, a few miles away. It was their plan to begin the procession at al-Azhar, the most respected seat of Islamic higher learning in the world, and end at the main Coptic cathedral to mourn and salute their Christian brethren. At the palpable height of sectarian suspicion, Heba and her cadre of loyal protesters were intent on disrupting that.

It was all too surreal and moving. As I watched the Muslim Heba lead protesters to a church to mourn the death of Christians a few days before, I was overtaken by an amalgam of pride and hope. Tears welled up in my eyes. I stood immobilized, enchanted by the sight. In my emotional daze, I felt a sudden and strong thrust to my back as I was tossed off the road and onto the nearby sidewalk.

"Be careful, *ya basha*," shouted a voice behind me. As I caught myself from falling, I turned around to see that a middle-aged man who wore his beard and white garb in the manner often associated with Salafis had pushed me out of the path of an oncoming vehicle. I was surprised and thankful. Throughout the march, he had volunteered to guard the protesters by guiding the flow of traffic around them, keeping them off the road, and making sure they were not attacked by thugs and hostile groups. I thanked him profusely. He nodded and dutifully returned to his navigational responsibilities. With one arm enveloping the marchers and his other fist in the air, he shouted "Muslim, Christian, one hand!"

As the procession crawled along, it came to a bottleneck leading into Abbasiya, a densely populated area that is home to the Ministry of Defense, and where recent flare-ups had occurred between protesters and supporters of SCAF. As we passed under a bridge, people emerged from the side streets, first out of curiosity and later in solidarity. The sound of the chant "Muslim, Christian, one hand!" amplified as it echoed off the buildings and the bridge overhead. Our feet became more confident and the stomping shook the ground.

Intent on documenting this unique procession, I raced ahead to its front. I needed to show friends and family that this country had not splintered and it had not bowed its head. I needed evidence to illustrate that its social fabric had not been torn, and that its unity was preserved even after the regime's attempts to sow discord between Egyptians. I took dozens of photographs. But what caught my attention most was a young woman who stood out in the crowd. She was the only person who was completely silent. She did not chant or shout. She spoke to no one. She wore nothing but black. And while everyone's sorrow and anger was palpable, her face radiated peace and tranquillity. She wore a pendant with a hologram engraved in the form of a young man's face. His long shaggy hair was tucked behind his ears. In this picture, he was smiling broadly from cheek to cheek. As I stared at her, someone noticed my fixated gaze, leaned over my shoulder, and whispered into my ear, "That's Mary, Mina Danial's sister."

October 9, 2011 is an unforgettable day in modern Egyptian history. Of course there are many landmark occasions to celebrate and mourn in the lifetime of a nation like Egypt's, whose seven-thousand-year lineage spans civilizations, dynasties, empires, cultures. And while two dates, January 25 and February 11, have both etched their place in just the last year—the first for the eruption of the revolution and the second for the toppling of Mubarak—2011 has been a year of almost daily sacrifice and bloodshed.

The Egyptian calendar has become filled with days to commemorate and remember. But on October 9, some eight months after Mubarak, the political fault lines in Egypt were redrawn, and the revolution was reignited.

Egypt's Christians, the majority belonging to the local Coptic Orthodox denomination, had spent the last thirty years in relative hibernation. They had retracted themselves from public life, grown increasingly insular, and lost trust in state institutions. They had delegated all social, cultural, religious, and political duties on their behalf to the Church. Their contribution to Egypt's history was being gradually omitted from the national curriculum, they became increasingly invisible, and the state rendered everything related to them an issue of national security. Using a combination of blackmail and fearmongering, the ruling National Democratic Party had effectively silenced them and ensured their full compliance. The government was guaranteed Christian loyalty by waving around the Muslim Brotherhood opposition as a bogeyman to scare them. In response, like all institutions in Egypt during Mubarak's era, including all ministries and al-Azhar, the Church actively disengaged its clergy and congregation from politics. As a minority with a 'special status,' they were taught to be cooperative, quiet, and, on all political matters, completely disengaged. So although they were facing the same predicaments as all Egyptians, many of them were indoctrinated to believe that remaining a spectator to events guarantees self-preservation. But some of them broke from that mold. History had taught these few that their community's suffering is greatest when they are disengaged from public life, not the opposite. Having committed myself to Egypt's prodemocracy movement some years ago, albeit from a distance since I resided in North America, I was always saddened by the modest turnout of Christians at protests and I had given up trying to compel other Copts to participate. Although I understood their fears and concerns, I was convinced that the emancipation of Egypt's minorities would come only in the context of an intertwined, multidenominational, unified, collective movement against the autocracy and corruption that disempowered Egyptians of all stripes.

When the revolution erupted, the Coptic Church, like al-Azhar, discouraged its adherents from joining the protest movement. Many disobeyed this call to stay home. On the first Friday of the revolution, January 28, 2011, the now infamous "Day of Rage," Christian protesters surrounded Muslim worshipers, and hand in hand, many bearing tattooed crosses on their wrists, guarded their Muslim brethren in Tahrir Square in the face of attacks from security forces and Mubarak's gangs. They did so for every prayer. When Mubarak was finally toppled, the country rejoiced as one—Muslim and Christian.

But it wasn't long before things got complicated. A revival of empowerment and feelings of heightened dignity reverberated across the country. Everyone demanded a better life as the revolution spread to every corner of the nation and trickled into every institution. The remnants of the old regime, which remained steadfast in retaining power, were being challenged, as attempts to dislodge it grew bolder. The state, now under the military rule, tried to counter this by describing all further demands as "factional" protests, arguing they were divisive rather than being in the whole nation's best interests. Factory strikes were "factional." Teachers' protests were "factional." Sit-ins demanding media freedom were "factional." Any protest by the Nubians of Upper Egypt, the Bedouins of Sinai or the Western Desert, or the Copts was painted as "factional," "sectarian," divisive, and opportunistic.

So when a largely Christian protest marched toward the state television building on October 9, 2011 to protest attacks against Coptic places of worship in various parts of the country and the failure of the government to protect them or exact justice against the perpetrators, SCAF was not in a mood to tolerate what they saw as insolent dissident behavior from a feeble, "factional" minority.

Among the peaceful procession of the young and old, rich and poor, was a shaggy-haired, twenty-year-old man with a childlike smile. Despite the somber mood of the march with many holding candles, this young man's face radiated with energy and optimism. His was a well-known face. It had been at most protests, from the early days of the revolution to marches against the military's rule during the transition period. Many of those who met him in Tahrir didn't know this young man was Christian. It did not matter. During a crescendo in the revolution, when Mubarak supporters galloped in on horses and camels armed with knives, swords, and batons to punish the revolutionaries in Tahrir, this young man joined his brethren in protecting the square and earned his battle wounds. In one photo taken on February 2, 2011, a medic can be seen removing a bullet from his leg. The young man is laughing off his wounds. If he could smile then, he can smile now, for he had seen worse days in the fight to remove Mubarak.

As the thousands-strong procession approached Maspero, something strange was in the air. Despite the orderly nature of the protest, the atmosphere was unusually tense. The television building toward which they were heading was heavily fortified by armored vehicles and military personnel. Everything was about to change in a minute's time. The sound of gunshots rang in the air and panic spread through the crowd. The soldier who typically stood idle in front of the building lifted his shield off the ground, adjusted his helmet, and raised his baton in the air. In an unexpected turn of events, hundreds of soldiers charged the crowd of protesters and attacked them senselessly, as if herding animals. Screams filled the air as people tried to rescue their friends and family from the hands of the men in uniform.

Out of the blue, an armored personnel carrier came racing through the crowd, swerving from side to side, as people scurried out of its way. Once it reached the end of the road, it turned around and accelerated back as it scraped the sides of parked cars. It was headed straight for the clusters of protesters. It veered onto and off the sidewalk in an attempt to plow into as many people as possible. Screams turned into wails as the blood of the bodies mowed down by the army vehicle flowed onto the street. Crushed torsos, flattened skulls, and body parts were scattered on the ground as people tried to identify the victims and help the injured in the dark night, while watching their backs for further attacks. As videos trickled in on that night and the following day, I watched this massacre unfold on the screen in utter disbelief. This unspeakable horror was practically unfathomable and wholly unexplainable. My body felt numb. I was left speechless for many hours. A sense of helplessness fell on me. The great Egyptian revolution at which the world rejoiced, that inspired similar movements in the region and beyond, and that international leaders raced to pay tribute to seemed to die before my eyes. In disbelief and denial, I was subconsciously mourning not only the lives of those lost in this carnage, but also the innocence of a once-utopian revolution.

Some seven hours later, when the bloodbath had come to an end, the Maspero massacre had claimed thirty-one lives. Once again, the same young man with the bushy hair had been involved in another attack by the tyrannical state on its people. Once again, he was a victim. Once again, he inspired those around him. Once again, despite the horror, his smile radiated stubbornly as if taunting fate. But this time, fate had called his name. His lifeless body lay on the cold hospital floor with two bullet holes. One had pierced his chest. The other entered the back of his head. His name was Mina Danial.

The ruling military junta had set a historic precedent and killed its own people in cold blood. They counted on the Muslim majority to overlook the massacre, and to support the military by condemning their Christian countrymen and -women. But they had miscalculated. Their foolish barbarism had stripped Mubarak's military of its camouflage, added to the ranks of the revolution's martyrs, and turned the young Christian man with a permanent smile, Mina Danial, into the new Khaled Said.

For months and years to come, the chant "*Iqtil Khalid, iqtil Mina, kul rusasa bitqawwina*" ("Kill Khalid, kill Mina, every bullet strengthens us") would be a rallying cry for unity between Muslims and Christians against tyranny. Today Mina Danial is immortalized on an Egyptian flag bearing the symbols of the crescent and cross interlinked alongside the word *hurriya* (freedom). Underneath the flag is a red fabric sheet with a stenciled image in his likeness. Since Mina's death, this flag was named after him, and has become an iconic symbol of the continuing revolution. Two young revolutionaries, Tarek al-Tayeb, a Muslim, and Michael Karara, a Christian, withstood tear gas, beatings, and rubber bullets for many days as they alternated waving the banner on the frontlines of battles between protesters and security forces.

When Egypt's military rulers inherited power from Mubarak, many hoped they would be the benevolent force that would shepherd the country toward democracy. But SCAF has dashed those hopes. Instead, they have taken pages out of Mubarak's playbook and used religion to drive a wedge between Muslims and Christians in the country. And in instances like the Maspero massacre, they have surpassed their predecessor in both brutality and impunity. As Egyptians called for justice, the military responded with arrogance and disregard. Despite the photographic and videographic evidence that incriminates the military police for the atrocities on October 9, the military has instead blamed the victims, accused the protesters of incitement, and washed its hands of any wrongdoing. They still hope to erase any memory of this crime and come out unscathed.

Egyptians often say that the worst criminal is "he who kills someone and walks in their funeral." On the first Coptic Christmas after the Maspero massacre, SCAF did just this. General Hamdi Badeen, the man who oversaw the conduct of the military police on that bloody night, sat in the front row at the mass and, smiling, shook hands with Pope Shenouda to congratulate Egypt's Christians. Many in the audience watched with disgust. And when the pope thanked SCAF for their "wise management" of the country, a few outraged youth interrupted the speech with screams of "Down, down with military rule!"

"*Yasqut, yasqut hukm al-'askar!*"

"*Yasqut, yasqut hukm al-'askar!*"

The army generals have tried to appease Christians since the Maspero massacre. Appearing to be the only supporters of Christian political representation, they appointed five Copts to Egypt's first post-Mubarak parliament. By so doing, SCAF expected silent consent from Egypt's Christians. By denying any wrongdoing, and procuring silence from everyone, SCAF was confident that national amnesia would absolve them.

Yet they had overlooked a new generation of Egyptians. We are proud, unrelenting, and indefatigable. Egypt is full of Hebas who will speak truth to power against all odds and in the face of the gravest danger. They had underestimated the humble yet confident power of a sister's quiet agony. And as if forgetting what it means to be soldiers, they had lost sight of how to defend our honor and dignity. By killing us in the name of stabilizing the country, they had broken the delicate social contract with us, the people. Once heralded as national heroes and defenders of the country, today they have inadvertently lost this honor. Now we, those with the least power and greatest conviction, are the only source of legitimacy. When they killed us at Maspero, and in subsequent incidents on Muhammad Mahmud Street, at the Cabinet sit-in, at the Port Said soccer massacre, and elsewhere, they repeated Mubarak's mistakes. The specters of those who are gone are greater than their living bodies. Egypt's rulers had once again underestimated a generation who, like Mina Danial, are the rightful bearers of Egypt's flag and whose yet-unwritten stories will break through the silence to unite a country in defiance of all odds. We might be an overly romantic, irrational, and unrealistic generation, but we are the future. And when we finally prevail, in *our* Egypt, as Caribbean poet Aimé Césaire put it, there will be "room for everyone at the rendezvous of victory."

Of Men and Hymen

December 25, 2011

Military rule in Egypt came to an end last week. It did not come at the hands of a powerful political adversary, a populist upris- ing, an internal coup d'état, an armed struggle by an insurgent group, or a foreign incursion. It was not the result of a judicial ruling, a legislative bill passed, or an international human rights resolution pushed. Sixty years of totalitarian militarism backed by drummed-up, blinding propaganda all came crumbling down in the blink of an eye. In the future, don't let anyone fool you into thinking that it was thanks to their back- room deal-making, alliance-building, heroism, demagoguery, strategic wiliness, or superior intellect. Instead mark the date, December 17, 2011, when the fortress began to crumble.

It happened in a matter of seconds near Tahrir, and had an amateur videographer not been on hand to capture it, we would have missed this historic moment. An unnamed faceless soldier in the armed forces raised his foot and with all his might brought it crashing down onto the almost- bare chest of a nameless, faceless young woman. Infinitely more powerful and resonant than the annual televised glorification of the military, or the compulsory school trips to the October War Panorama, or the frequent press conferences to polish the brass, the girl, whose sole identification is the blue bra she wore, nailed the coffin of a stubborn, decrepit regime. Nothing about the account needs to be confirmed, corroborated, or inves- tigated. It simply is what it is.

She is the last of a long lineage of victims of this ruthless regime. In fact, just eleven months prior, several women protesters were captured from Tahrir, hauled to the grounds of the Egyptian Museum, and forced to strip before a medical staffer. His task was to lay his eyes and hands on their most protected of places in the name of examining their dignity and honor. He was to confirm and report whether their hymens were intact. And in doing so he had effectively raped them. The thin purposeless membrane was what they were reduced to. It did not matter what brought them to Tahrir, what they stood for, what they demanded, or their vision for the country. It did not matter that just a month earlier, they were being celebrated as the youth revolutionaries that toppled the dictator. It did not matter that these were fearless women who withstood tear gas and birdshot and faced live ammunition.

What did matter was to break their will, shatter their conscience, and extinguish their drive to fight on. Rape has long been utilized as a weapon of war, and for Samira Ibrahim and others, the virginity tests should have been a deathblow. Although most young women would be too humiliated to face the violation publicly, Samira did what the men in fatigues least expected. She came out in the media, recounted her experience in graphic detail, and faced off, single-handedly, against Egypt's highest powers. She held her hymen up high as if it were a flag for everyone to see. Whatever shame, embarrassment, and disgrace she was meant to feel she reflected back at SCAF and the military establishment. She had knocked down a wall in their once-immune citadel.

So when thousands-strong women's protests descended on Tahrir Square a few days ago, the mood was palpably angry. The often mis-characterized Egyptian woman—subservient, obedient, agreeable, coy, and extremely private—shattered this and every other myth about her. Unlike every other women's protest since the toppling of Mubarak, which were attacked by mobs of harassers, thugs, sexually deprived males, and depraved misogynists, this march's mood was explosive and furious. Dozens of women carried graffiti posters featuring a cartoon by Andeel of an angry young woman being approached by a uniformed arm with the powerful inscription "Your hand will be cut!"

As a deterrent for future action of this sort, this may have been a minor success for women's action in Egypt. However, the actions of the powerful help entrench a culture of violence against women and impunity for those who commit these actions.

And while the oppressive uniformed folks are easily recognizable and now on the verge of being conquered, it is the everyday plain-clothed adversary that is most worrying and disturbing. A combination of con-tradictory messages on gender identities and relations in Egypt helped foster a schizophrenic concoction of sexism and women's empowerment in the public domain. Suzanne Mubarak's half-hearted, top-down and elitist campaigns to uplift women resulted in a bipolar experience. While on the one hand campaigns to fight female genital mutilation led to its medicalization rather than eradication, Egyptian mothers until only recently could not pass on their citizenship to their children. Efforts were made to increase employment for women, but no considerations were made to ensure pay equivalence with men. In fact, the women who occupied the highest level in the state were all effectively enslaved to the Mubaraks. It was not unusual to find some of the women ministers kissing Suzanne's hands as an act of complete submission and supplication.

As marriage rates dwindle, wages drop, prospects decline, and overall frustration mounts, we are witnessing a spike in hostility toward women. With harassment as a cornerstone of such violations, the situation has become so dire that virtually no public space is completely threat-free. The overt and adamant masculinization of public space is itself an act of violence against women. It must be said that the rise in Islamist fervor, particularly of the Salafi brand, in Egyptian society has fostered an ethical gauge and behavioral barometer for women. A new rhetoric that advocates separation between the sexes, growing imposition of what are seen as 'signs of religiosity' and 'modesty,' and a deafening chorus of quiet acceptance of predicament and custom—religious or cultural—have all exacerbated the condition of women in the post-Mubarak moment.

This is especially telling as it coincides with a dramatic transformation in the demographics of employment in the country. More and more women have entered the workforce in the past twenty years and in some sectors, such as government, actually exceed men. In fact, between ages forty and fifty, there are more women working than men. This is a substantial shift in the country's gender dynamics, as many women are the sole providers in their households. So whether it is a feeling of emasculation on the part of Egyptian men that causes them to undermine women, false expectation that such behaviors as harassment are endearing, a rampant culture of impunity, or mounting sexual frustration, men now feel increasingly entitled to impose on women.

And while every act of subordination imposed on a woman is a violation of her honor, the irony is that this very subordination is done in the name of honor. It is this same honor that SCAF member Ismail Etman claimed to be guarding when he sent his men hymen-hunting. It is the same honor that many a Salafi shaykh used, not to defend, but to decry the "blue bra girl" when she was stripped and stomped in Tahrir.

It would be a mistake to think this struggle is not about women's bodies. It is also a mistake to assume this struggle is entirely about women's bodies. In its most holistic sense, it is overarchingly about power. And with the locus of power constantly in flux, it is difficult to tell which way the pendulum will settle once it stops swinging. And when it does, if the emancipation of women is not a central consideration, then we can bid this revolution adieu.

The Lost Tribe

March 1, 2012

Karim left Egypt in 1992 with no intention of returning. By the time the revolution erupted, almost two decades later, his Egyptian passport had long since expired, he had become a naturalized American, he had married a Venezuelan, and his Arabic was now hesitant and accented. Egypt had become a distant memory, a symbol of a long-gone past, a country associated not with fond experiences but with corruption, degradation, and ill fate. Like hundreds of thousands of Egyptians, Karim left his country during the Mubarak era on a one-way trip to a better life. And a better life it was. The thirty-five-year-old finance consultant had little to complain about. But something happened on that fateful day in January. Watching the revolution unfold on American television, something rumbled within. Karim felt a sense of estrangement, the awakening of a deeply entrenched longing, a rekindling of what had been lost.

His Facebook messages went from mundane daily life-in-the-suburbs-type posts to furor and anxiety about a land thousands of kilometers away. He felt like a zombie going to work every day after consecutive sleepless nights spent glued to streaming videos from Tahrir and reruns of Egyptian television programs. No one he knew understood his anguish, his concern, his worry. When Mubarak left, the Egyptian inside him was reborn. Beaming with pride, he was on a quest to fill in the two-decade gap in his relationship with Egypt, and a visit was finally in order.

But the return of the prodigal son would be delayed, as jubilation turned to dismay turned to fear turned to tyranny. He was heartbroken as he watched Egypt's revolution suffocate at the hands of SCAF. It seemed there was little more to celebrate, yet he could no longer return to the innocent naiveté of the blissfully ignorant. Eventually his wife, Cristina, in an attempt to settle his unrest, urged him to spend the Thanksgiving vacation in Egypt. It was to coincide with the first round of a historic post-Mubarak parliamentary election.

Forty-eight hours after arrival, Karim and Cristina would find themselves at the epicenter not of a victory celebration but of a revolution-in-progress. In Tahrir Square, they were at the heart of the battles of Muhammad Mahmud Street: ambulances, tear gas, rubber bullets, blood, perseverance, heroism, and pain. Karim was a changed man. Something inside him would never be the same. There are hundreds of thousands of Karims out there, the 'lost tribe' of exiled Egyptians, who watched and felt the revolution rumble inside them despite the separation. I met a professor at Cairo University who, in a surge of hope, left his respectable professorial position in Japan to return and teach in Egypt. However, eight months after the fall of Mubarak, his enthusiasm was muted and his optimism subdued.

At a time when Egypt could have benefited significantly from the untapped resources and expertise of its newly engaged, fiercely loyal, and deeply committed diaspora, instead many of them have been driven away. Not only has the revolution been derailed so badly that the spirit of accomplishment has been practically drowned, the state has systematically and institutionally deployed xenophobia in much of its rhetoric. Egyptians abroad are part of an incomprehensibly complex and utterly illogical conspiracy to undermine the country and to lay the grounds for renewed imperialism, incitement against the military, and Coptic claims for equality.

There are plenty of reasons for Egyptians abroad to feel demoralized by their binationalism. A rumor circulated that an administrative court had annulled liberal representative Amr Hamzawi's membership in the parliament because he holds German citizenship. The same thing happened a month before the revolution began in 2010, when ElBaradei was accused of concealing Austrian nationality to make himself eligible for presidential candidacy. The first signs of this in-group/out-group dynamic came with the constitutional amendments referendum, which stipulated that any candidate for president must have Egyptian parents who never acquired any other citizenship in their life, and cannot be married to someone other than an Egyptian citizen. One can imagine this condition being an obstacle for many qualified candidates in the forthcoming elections and the attempts of many a prominent politician to conceal his national heritage.

On April 7, 2011, less than two months after the toppling of Mubarak, with enthusiasm at its highest, I was invited to speak on a panel with Wael Ahmed Kamal Abu-l-Naga, Egypt's ambassador to Canada, at Ottawa University. When pressed on the issue of the right to vote, he argued that it would be impractical and unfathomable for Egyptians abroad to vote in the elections. A few weeks later, in protests at embassies worldwide, hyphenated Egyptians gathered to demand their right to vote in their country's elections. In Washington, D.C. they shouted "*Masri, masri hatta mamati*" (Egyptian, Egyptian until my death) as they demanded the vote in the parliamentary elections. It was in fact through the dedicated efforts of Egyptians in North America, Western Europe, Australia, and everywhere but the Arab world that SCAF and the interim government were pressured to accept and comply with the court ruling to allow Egyptians abroad to vote. It was not the Egyptians in the Gulf, whose mere participation in a chapter of the National Association for Change (NAC) in Kuwait cost them their jobs and led to their deportation. In the end, it was the effort of the protesters, activists, and campaigners based in the west who won for Egyptians everywhere the chance to vote. And while the majority of voters outside Egypt are in Saudi Arabia, followed by other Gulf countries, it is clear that those who pushed most for this recognition benefited the least.

On December 24, instead of staying home to enjoy their Christmas Eve day off, they braved the winter weather to protest outside a virtually empty Egyptian Military Defense office in Washington, D.C. against SCAF's mistreatment of protesters in and around Tahrir Square, and to demand an end to military rule. Some of their chants were statements condemning U.S. support for SCAF and calling for an end of funding and support, without excusing U.S. action or intervention.

The recent attack on NGOs by SCAF on the grounds of receiving foreign funding reflects the bipolarity of the military's relationship with both the United States and civil society. Understandably, legal measures should govern a foreign country's spending in the domestic affairs of another, especially in the political arena. However, the manner in which SCAF managed this particular case was not only alarmist and exaggerated, it was also clearly a public relations campaign and a slap on the United States' wrist for speaking too loudly about SCAF's management of the transition. And when push came to shove, SCAF slipped the American defendants out of the country and acted sheepish to the Egyptian press. In doing so they have targeted all Egyptian progressive and liberal voices abroad and inside the country under the guise of being pro-western or acting in the interest of the United States, all while camouflaging the reality that Egypt's military receives more American aid than any other institution in the country and is annually among the top four recipients of American military aid. And sadly, most calls for SCAF's accountability are seen as jeopardizing the stability agenda advocated by the west.

Obviously one should not advocate for the kind of naiveté that overlooks the growing roles and competing interests of international powers and regional hegemons in Egypt, but the discourse coming out of SCAF and the interim government, along with their foot soldiers in the state media and pro-military private networks, warrants criticism from all. They oscillate between two positions—the foreigner complex (u'dit al-kha-waga), which sees the foreigner as desirable and superior, and xenophobia (unsuriya), which demonizes the foreigner out of suspicion and fear. Egypt post-Mubarak is being pulled in opposite directions, between the global and the provincial, between self-orientalizing and self-occidentalizing. By appealing to the masses, SCAF is using ignorance to sponsor an attack against bourgeois sensibilities without a corrective bias to support the subjugated and disadvantaged. Quite the contrary: SCAF has effectively strengthened the hand of the bourgeoisie by forgoing any action on economic redistribution.

What the Egyptian state has fostered for at least a generation is a deep suspicion of the world, despite its citizens' dire need to engage with it. Egyptians have grown to despise and distrust the west while lining up at its embassies to seek visas. The overlooked issue is that most of the Egyptians who left the country departed to seek better opportunities as jobs dwindled at home. For over seventy years, the country's brain drain has been quite severe. While more people have been educated, the system has deteriorated at an astonishing rate. Employment opportunities have dropped significantly, forcing qualified workers to seek jobs and better lives elsewhere. Some have died in their pursuit of greener pastures beyond Egypt's border, such as those who have drowned in ferry accidents traveling to and from the Gulf countries. It is thought that the total number of Egyptians abroad may be as high as 8 million.

Shockingly, the total number of those who have registered to vote from outside Egypt is only around 300,000. According to the election committee website, 142,000 of those registered are in Saudi Arabia, 73,000 in Kuwait, 36,000 in the United Arab Emirates, over 21,000 in Qatar,

20,000 in the United States, and 9,000 in Canada. More Egyptians registered from Qatar than from the United States. In the end, the most active and dynamic diasporic communities politically are, ironically, the least represented in voting weight. Over time this has resulted in dwindling enthusiasm for participating in Egyptian public life. While the number of Egyptians in the United States who became newly engaged politically in their home country was extremely high as a result of the revolution, this excitement quickly waned.

The calls for voting rights abroad echoed loudly until it became evident that SCAF and the ruling political forces were no longer committed to true democracy, killing the expatriates' will to participate. Egyptians abroad watched as their country descended from one failure to the next. They watched as one piece of bad news followed the next. They watched while the constitutional referendum was concocted swiftly to create rifts in Egyptian society. They watched as one protest after the next was broken up violently by the police and the new military authority. They watched as the revolutionaries moved from the squares to military jails one after the other. And they watched the military's vehicles crush protesters in plain view. At once, those Egyptians who felt a sense of nostalgia about their country and felt inspired by the courage of its youth quickly lost their faith in the revolution and those who claimed to have protected it.

The Three-Horned Bull

May 30, 2012

B eing a non-smoker in Cairo is a tiring experience. Never mind the inhalation of suffocating fumes from vehicle exhausts and hovering industrial smog or the annual mass combustion of rice chaff that sends a colossal billowing cloud over the city. Never mind the lack of concern and consideration for clean air in public spaces, even in the presence of infants and pregnant women. Never mind the fact that most locally manufactured tobacco products are notoriously packed with synthetic impurities and toxicants (as if tar and nicotine weren't enough!). Being a non-smoker is most endangering when a stranger—say, a taxi driver—stretches his arm to offer you that potent cigarette: To take or not to take. To take the cigarette is to violate one's own personal choice, subject one's body to a nefarious substance, douse one's clothes with a lingering unpleasant aroma, and submit one's will to external pressure. To refuse the cigarette is to turn down an act of hospitality and goodwill, break a social code, or imply that one is too classist to smoke with the 'masses,' or it may be seen as a sign of timidity, cowardice, and even emasculation. Quite a lot to process in a single decision, but nevertheless, it is a dilemma.

Egyptians are faced with such dilemmas on a ceaseless basis. Take the Sixth of October Bridge or Salah Salem Street during rush hour. Boycott mobile phone operator Mobinil because of Sawiris's Twitter joke, Vodafone for trying to take credit for the revolution, or Emirati Etisalat for its aggressive attempts to monopolize the Egyptian mobile-phone market. What to give up because one's salary is too minuscule to cover basic necessities? Food or medicine? Such are dilemmas, circumstances where two equally unfavorable and disadvantageous choices must be pondered and where inaction is not an option. This kind of philosophical conundrum is often described as "being on the horns of a dilemma," where one is faced with the outcome of "being impaled" by one of the two horns of a metaphorical bull.

Today Egypt is facing an even more puzzling predicament: a presidential trilemma. With the official results from the election confirming that the Muslim Brotherhood's Muhammad Morsi and Mubarak's last prime minister, Ahmad Shafiq, are heading toward a runoff, many Egyptians are gripped with a deep-seated sense of sunken disbelief, anxiety, panic, dejection, and demoralization. Shafiq is now effectively viewed as the military's strongman, an apologist for Mubarak's regime, and an unrelenting bulwark of the 'stability' camp. Revolutionaries see him as a Darth Vader character, whom they hold at least indirectly responsible for the surreal, murderous attack of February 2–3, 2011 on Tahrir, known unflatteringly as the "Battle of the Camel."

Morsi is the uncharismatic, unimaginative, unappealing, and often unintelligible *stibn* (spare tire) candidate for the Muslim Brotherhood, whose organization has alienated a large proportion of the population. By using religious rhetoric to elbow out political opposition during all three elections—constitutional amendments, parliamentary, and presidential—they have appeared opportunistic and disingenuous. Perhaps more catastrophically, their confusingly unclear rhetoric on whether they will impose *sharia* and their seemingly complicit silence during the killings of protesters in Maspero, Muhammad Mahmud, the Cabinet sit-in, Port Said, and Abbasiya, all in just seven short months, have left many Egyptians concerned about their trustworthiness. Not to mention their monopolization of the parliament and its most crucial legislative task ahead: the writing of the constitution.

Some appeals of the results are still outstanding, and a court is still reviewing whether former regime figures should be prevented from participating in political life (which may disqualify Shafiq). If the results stand, Egyptians will go to the ballot boxes in two weeks to choose between Shafiq and Morsi—a return to the old corrupt tyrannical regime or a complete transformation into a seemingly unfavorable scenario that would give the Brotherhood a complete trifecta of both parliamentary houses and the presidency. Throw in a few ingredients to raise both stakes and fears, such as sectarianism, and the bull's horns seem sharper than ever. With a number of people claiming that many Christians may have voted for Shafiq, there is a growing sentiment that the Coptic minority is anti-revolutionary, anti-Islamist, and pro–military council, making them the target of everyone but the supporters of the old regime.

In the few days between voting and the announcements of the results, there was absolute silence from the Presidential Elections Commission, which governs the process. With no official results disclosed, and with speculation and panic mounting, many were suspicious that something was being cooked up behind the scenes. Presidential candidates Abd al-Mun'im Abu al-Futuh, Hamdeen Sabbahi, and Amr Moussa all took advantage of this circumstance to file official complaints with the commission, calling for suspension, cancellation, a recount, or a freezing of the election in hope that their chances might be resuscitated. There was strong evidence suggesting fraud may have occurred, but the commission, which possesses absolute authority to refuse appeals or dismiss them outright without investigation, did precisely that.

In the meantime, it appears that the Supreme Council of the Armed Forces—the body that appointed the commission—was weighing its options with respect to the three candidates, including Sabbahi, who was only slightly lagging behind Shafiq in the official count.

Having butted heads with the Brotherhood ahead of this election, the council is less inclined to see Morsi go through, compared with the SCAF lackey Shafiq. Nevertheless, they almost certainly fear that a Shafiq win will start another wave of massive protests by the Islamists, secularists, revolutionaries, and other groups that would continue to prolong Egypt's 'transition' and hurt their already tarnished image internationally.

What would a Morsi presidency look like? With SCAF at the helm of Egypt's foreign policy, delicately balancing relations with the country's two top benefactors, the United States and Saudi Arabia, how would having the Brotherhood in the driver's seat affect these relations?

The Brotherhood has always been a thorn in the side for both Saudi Arabia and the United States. But recently this seems to be changing as congenial relations with Washington have emerged, delegates sent back and forth, and promises of compliance made. On the regional front, with Saudi Arabia dangling a hefty $3 billion grant that Egypt so desperately needs (especially because Fayza Abu'l-Naga, the international cooperation and planning minister, seems to be juggling the International Monetary Fund and World Bank), SCAF is inclined to do whatever the kingdom demands, even if it comes down to knocking the Brotherhood out. But luckily for Morsi and company, a recent diplomatic spat between Egypt and the Saudis ended with a top delegation comprising highest-level Brothers, such as People's Assembly speaker Saʿd al-Katatni, and other prominent Islamists traveling to Riyadh to genuflect and sing King Abdullah's praises. This may be just enough to ensure that the two giants, the United States and Saudi Arabia, turn a blind eye to a Morsi ascendancy.

The Muslim Brotherhood challenged any calls for a recount or investigation of irregularity for fear that this may disadvantage its candidate, either by dropping him from the second round or by introducing a less polarizing figure than Shafiq who would pose a greater challenge for Morsi. Alternatively, if fraud was indeed widespread (presumably to give Shafiq an advantage), the Brotherhood should instead be at the head of the pack in confronting it, for fear that it might repeat itself in the runoff, certainly to their disadvantage.

With both options for president presenting seemingly ominous outcomes for the electorate (not simply in their own persons, but in the resulting configuration of political forces and the ensuing realities), the hiatus and voting patterns have presented an unlikely possibility, a third wheel if you will: Hamdeen Sabbahi. A surprise success in the election, the Nasserist candidate who was virtually unknown to most Egyptians just a few months ago was able to secure substantial numbers and win huge metropolitan areas like Cairo, Alexandria (a Salafi stronghold), Port Said, Suez, and Giza. With a shabby, underfunded campaign and limited television spots during the run-up to the vote, Sabbahi seems to have soared precisely because of the lackluster image, overexposure, and polarizing rhetoric of the other candidates. Either way, he became an instant sensation once the results suggested Morsi and Shafiq had come out on top. Since then, he has been a sought-after television guest, and Egyptians flocked to support him online and in rallies, all hoping he may be vindicated with admission into the second round.

But Sabbahi is not without his quirks. With the deep state digging into the very viscera of Egyptian politics, is there no suspicion in his unexplainable glowing success? Is it possible that he may in fact be the one groomed to arrive on a white horse to sweep a runoff against Morsi by unifying revolutionaries, the poor, the wealthy, the liberal and secular, the Islamists, the former regime, and everyone but the Brotherhood, all while not alarming SCAF?

It is no surprise that as people sat before their televisions lamenting the dilemma of a Shafiq–Morsi duel, al-Nahar TV hosted Sabbahi in an interview that is nothing short of a breakthrough, akin to Wael Ghoneim's epic interview with Mona El Shazly on Dream TV in February 2011. The host, already calling him "Mr. President," could not stop basking in his glow, as prerecorded interviews with prominent revolutionaries and residents of his town spoke about him in near-messianic terms. The interview even included emotionally charged moments with carefully chosen background music to add to the melodrama, and frequent camera dissolves from videos to close-ups of Sabbahi wiping away his tears. This was a moment made for television. Sabbahi may have already won the nation's heart, and done so almost effortlessly. If he is a revolutionary, which he certainly seems to be, will he be able to confront SCAF on their violations? If he is a true Nasserist, will he see to it that the military establishment goes unchallenged, as did his inspiration? Arguably, this may be SCAF's best-case scenario. If they push Sabbahi back into the race, in one fell swoop they will have silenced the revolutionaries, liberals, Islamists, *fulul* (regime remnants), rich, poor, young, and old, thereby guaranteeing an end to public dissent and accordingly reducing scrutiny and allowing state institutions time and space to ossify. Could Sabbahi be another horn of the bull, likely to poke Egyptians?

Egyptians have known and understood the classic definition of 'dilemma' from time immemorial, and have immortalized it in their use of the word *khazuq*, meaning 'an instrument used to impale.' Some say that when Egyptians came out to protest, they were choosing between the *khazuq* of Mubarak's police and the *khazuq* of uncertainty. They have since tasted *khazuq*s from SCAF, the police, the government, the Brotherhood, the Salafis, the liberal parties, the disjointed youth revolutionaries, the economy, the religious institutions, and other Egyptians as well. As people's dislike for both Shafiq and Morsi deepens, and with Sabbahi's popularity continuing to soar, many are praying for a miracle. Yet there is no good outcome. Instead, it is between bad and worse. All things equal, if the status quo continues, we should all take a collective deep breath and brace for the pain. And the next time you're offered a cigarette in a Cairo taxi, be sure to take it.

3

AD INFINITUM

Damn you, silence! My dream will not die!
If they chained my stride, I still have a voice
If they dragged me every day and stripped me with their oppression
If their bullets killed me, I still won't accept silence
Press the trigger, aim, fire, and kill
My chest is wide open to you! I will continue!
      —Ana Masri Band, "Damn You, Silence" (December 2011)

We are the leader we have been waiting for.
      —Spray-painted on a wall in Cairo by graffiti artist Keizer

The Conscientious Objectors

June 16, 2012

In August 1966, during the Vietnam War, when the United States was embroiled in a deep and lengthy conflict, a young fighter with considerable renown and popularity across the world became persona non grata for refusing to take part in his "national duty" and go to the front lines. Muhammad Ali was a rising star in the boxing world when the draft called him to join the troops in Southeast Asia, but he broke with protocol when he declared that war is against the teaching of the Qur'an, and put himself on a legal and moral collision course with the state and the public. In doing so, he joined the ranks of a growing number of young men and women who took a stance against the war. In a state where their refrain was deemed illegal, they were publicly known as conscientious objectors. The term itself is ironic since it suggests that one is just, upright, honest, faithful, and devoted while standing trial for violation of the law.

Muhammad Ali was eventually acquitted. He would also live to see his decision vindicated not just from a personal standpoint but from a collective national one, as the country went through a reevaluation of the conflict in Vietnam.

Today, the Egyptian electorate faces a struggle not unlike that of the young boxer. With the majority not falling into the categories of Muslim Brotherhood supporters or former regime sympathizers, choosing between Ahmad Shafiq and Muhammad Morsi in the second round of the presidential elections has turned into a moral minefield. The unflattering choice of a complete monopoly by the Brotherhood of all but one branch of government versus the reconstitution of Hosni Mubarak's old guard has catapulted an increasingly popular third option onto the scene—the boycott option.

Not unlike conscientious objectors, the boycott camp has been subjected to perhaps the most vicious attacks from both ends of the election spectrum, as they are described in the same terms as those who refused the military draft. As is the case with all election boycott campaigns, its participants are always met with fervent accusatory defamation, from claims of disloyalty and lack of patriotism to "dishonoring one's country." In the case of revolutionary Egypt, intentionally not voting or voiding one's vote is seen at best as a deplorable act akin to leading the country into a dark abyss, and at worst desecrating the memory of the revolution's martyrs.

Not seeing one's candidate in the runoff is rarely justifiable grounds for a boycott. And in the case of the runoff between Shafiq and Morsi, this isn't the thrust of the argument for Egypt's boycotters. Instead it is a deep-seated conviction that the anomaly is not in the choices but in the structure of the system. What was built on a mistake can only be erroneous. In the end, this is an election devoid of legal legitimacy from conception to execution. Nevertheless, the Egyptian electorate has been forced to sleepwalk their way through the voting process as if walking the plank toward outcomes already vetted by the ruling Supreme Council of the Armed Forces.

In the end, despite the likelihood of displeasure with the election outcome, we should not expect that either Shafiq or Morsi will create a cataclysmic change in the way politics in Egypt will function. The fear, concern, worry, and absolute paranoia are palpable. Suspicions that Shafiq will prove to be a more diabolical dictator than his predecessor and use violence gratuitously, or that Morsi will turn Egypt into Afghanistan, are quite ungrounded. Both candidates are more likely to pragmatically oppose the continuation of revolutionary action and support a status quo that affirms stability at all costs.

For all intents and purposes, the election boycott doesn't need a campaign to gather support. Egyptians have already been observing it. From the constitutional referendum vote in March 2011 until the presidential election in June 2012, the voter turnout across the country has steadily dropped despite the greater visibility of the campaigns and the rising stakes. Although the boycott in Egypt won't achieve remarkable success, such as Jamaica's in 1983 when the voter turnout was a laughable 2.7 percent (which kept the incumbent party in power for several years), elections under military rule have already lost their stamina.

We must come to terms with a new reality: that revolutionary Egypt is simply ungovernable. The country is no longer what Mubarak touted as a "nation of institutions." With institutional failure came self-government—Egyptians often say "*al-balad mashya bi-l-baraka*" (the country's running on blind luck). The state has choked on both its own incompetence and the revolution, and Egyptians have taken it upon themselves to reconstitute their own state outside of power. The best example of this is that the seven-month disappearance of the police force in Egypt did not result in a complete collapse of the public order. Whether Egyptians go to the polls or avoid them in these days is not a testament to their enthrallment with the process or their faith in the system, but rather a performance that fails to hide their displeasure with those they elect. Now that SCAF has effectively repossessed the reigns of legislative power in the country, the last nail has been hammered into the coffin of any electoral legitimacy under the junta. A word of advice for Egypt's next "elected" president: Whether or not we dip our fingers in the dye today, we are all conscientious objectors.

Morsi's Debts

June 26, 2012

For sixteen months, SCAF has tried to convince us we are indebted to them for the revolution. In reality it was the military council that was indebted to us for its newfound absolute powers. Today, there's enough debt to go around. The Salafis owe to the revolution their historic political rise and their escape from the noose of Mubarak's state security. The country's liberals owe SCAF and the judiciary for the disqualification of Hazim Abu Ismail from the presidential roster. The military is indebted to the Muslim Brotherhood for their silent obedience throughout a year of violence against protesters and revolutionaries. The Brotherhood owes the non-Islamist revolutionaries for kick-starting the uprising last year. All of this debt, while the country is running in the red. Virtually no single political institution, party, organization, group, state apparatus, or movement possesses a reservoir of absolute legitimacy in the current maelstrom.

Yet the one person whose debts are most colossal is the newly minted president Muhammad Morsi. Many a commentator, and Morsi himself, have admitted that even if he possessed the executive power (recently stripped from him by SCAF's constitutional declaration supplement), the tasks of balancing the economy, uniting the Egyptian public, managing the country's increasingly entangled foreign policy, and, most importantly, enacting directives that fulfill the revolution's goals of subsidies, dignity, freedom, and social justice, appear insurmountable. But even all of these challenges do not obscure his greatest burden. Like Atlas from the Greek myth, who was condemned to carry the celestial universe (depicted in art as the earth), on his shoulders for eternity, Morsi carries into his amputated presidential post a universe of unpayable debts.

Morsi's greatest creditor is of course the Muslim Brotherhood, for nurturing him throughout much of his political and professional career and for pulling him, in a gesture of revelation, out of near-obscurity to lead their charge to the presidential palace. He owes Khairat al-Shater, the Brotherhood behemoth, for relinquishing the spotlight to him and entrusting him with this task following his disqualification from the race. Even before he exited the race, al-Shater held a press conference where he presented Morsi as the second candidate, describing him as "a better choice than myself." Morsi cannot forget the organization's investment of tens of millions of pounds (if not more) and the dedication of tens of thousands of its loyalists to energize his campaign at a time when many of his competitors, such as Sabbahi, Abu al-Futuh, Khaled Ali, and Hisham al-Bastawisi, had to struggle to solicit meager contributions. He owes the Brotherhood's Supreme Guide, Muhammad Badi', for exercising his authority and dominion to bestow his blessing and allow him to be the face of a long-awaited Brotherhood presidency. Not only did the organization nurture him personally, it made his unlikely meteoric rise into politics possible by harvesting him from its ranks. That is why we should see Morsi's public "departure" from the Brotherhood, and his resignation from the leadership of the Freedom and Justice Party (FJP) before becoming president, as a farfetched and unconvincing gimmick.

A significant proportion of Morsi's deficit is owed to the ruling SCAF, with whom he has been playing a game of rhetorical brinksmanship over the past few weeks. Both have flexed their muscles before arriving at a seemingly conciliatory conclusion. Arguably, SCAF could have disqualified Morsi from eligibility for any number of reasons, actual or contrived, as they did with other candidates prior to the election. Additionally, lest we be fooling ourselves, the Presidential Elections Commission (PEC), in addition to being absolute and incontestable in its rulings, was also appointed by the military council. There are at least five scenarios the PEC could have orchestrated to disadvantage Morsi significantly, including the disqualification of Shafiq, which would have fielded an arguably more competitive contender, or disbarring Morsi on the grounds of illegal campaigning by the Brotherhood and the Freedom and Justice Party. But none of these things happened. Furthermore, SCAF also appeared to forgo a confrontation with the Brotherhood at a time when the military seemed to have gained electoral power, buoyed by Shafiq's 48 percent vote. At Hike Step military base on Saturday afternoon, in what was dubbed a "transfer-of-power" ceremony, SCAF reminded Morsi in not-so-subtle ways that had it not been for the generals, Egypt would not be where it is now, and by extension, neither would Morsi. So in the end, Morsi is president not simply because of the electoral win, but with a nod from SCAF—a debt he will have to repay.

And if that weren't enough, perhaps Morsi's greatest debt is to the electorate outside of the Muslim Brotherhood, whose support catapulted him past his opponent. To Egypt's revolutionary groups and individuals, from the April 6 Youth Movement to the Ultras groups, from Wael Ghoneim to the once-demonized Revolutionary Socialists, Morsi's diametrically opposed camp is extremely wide and polarized, pushing him beyond his comfort zone, his Brotherhood base. Many of these groups "squeezed a lemon over themselves" (an Egyptian adage meaning that they bit their tongues and acted against their natural inclination) and voted for Morsi in order to defeat the old regime. They did so despite the unappealing and often counterrevolutionary record of the Muslim Brotherhood throughout the transition, where they abandoned the protesters during their bloody confrontations with security forces between March 2011 and February 2012. With Morsi having won seven million new votes in the second round compared to the first, most of these voters had clearly preferred other candidates over him but supported him nonetheless, hoping he would deliver. They represent more than half of his voters and to them he owes his presidency. This non–Muslim Brotherhood electorate that entrusted Morsi with its vote expects to be rewarded for its support.

In his first few days, Morsi has said what he needed to say. In meetings with families of the martyrs, including Mina Danial's sister, he acknowledged that the Maspero attacks and subsequent violence under SCAF should not be concealed or overlooked. He has also begun to genuflect to SCAF by making public overtures to the council's "wise management" of the post-Mubarak transition. Even on the controversial issue of where to take the presidential oath—in the heart of revolutionary Tahrir, before the now-defunct People's Assembly in protest, or in the same constitutional court that dissolved the elected body—Morsi went bipolar. Asserting his revolutionary tendencies, he participated in an electrifying mock swearing-in on a stage in Tahrir as if to spite SCAF, then politely and obediently succumbed to their will the next day to be officially confirmed as president before the constitutional court. In a single surreal and eclectic day, Morsi ceremoniously implied his authority over the armed forces at Cairo University and a few hours later, at Hike Step military base, he hesitated and retracted the word "order" when addressing SCAF's high brass. As the president becomes a more adept and charismatic performer with every engagement, so has his ability to circumvent confrontation by speaking out of both sides of his mouth. This ambivalence should force the revolution's proponents to take heed and judge Morsi on his actions rather than his words.

At this critical juncture, as SCAF tightens its grip on power and hardens its once flaccid coup in an attempt to emasculate the new president, the unaffiliated revolutionary masses are hopeful Morsi can stand tall and repay his outstanding debts to them rather than obey his elder Brothers or genuflect to the men in uniform.

Year of the Ostrich

July 1, 2012

In April 1954, less than two years after the military ousted King Faruq's monarchy, it became apparent that the men in uniform would not be relinquishing power in Egypt. The Free Officers' coup d'état paved the way for the constitution of the Revolutionary Command Council (RCC), a supra-legal body with executive, legislative, and judicial power wielded over every branch of government including the media. Before the RCC decided to exercise its hegemony and muzzle any criticism in the media, there was a twenty-month period where Egypt's press flourished. During this transition period, General Muhammad Naguib, the most senior officer among the coup's leaders, had committed to surrender power to civilian control, relegating Egypt's military to a non-sovereign role in the post-transition period, and encouraging public deliberation over these issues in the press. This plan would not come to fruition. The wiggle room ceased abruptly as the RCC grew increasingly comfortable atop the food chain. To silence dissent against their ascent to power, the RCC would have to reform Egypt's media once and for all. Such an abrupt action, clearly inconsistent with their original claims of press openness, would have to be justified politically. By elbowing Naguib out of the picture, Gamal Abd al-Nasser and the remaining officers turned to the renewed threat of western imperialism and the neighboring adversary in Israel to explain the need for a centralized media system. The continued injustice of settler colonialism in Israel, as well as a hardened Anglo-Franco-American stance toward the new administration, was treated as grounds to warrant vigilance, unanimity, commitment, and obedience from Egypt's press corps. Anwar al-Sadat would be tasked with overseeing much of this process of "press rehabilitation." He set up the self-proclaimed "revolution's paper" *al-Gumhuriya*, created the protocols that made state media completely submissive to the military's directives, seduced and coerced all of Egypt's independent press into compliance, and used nepotism, intimidation, and competition to extinguish the flame of introspection and inquiry among journalists and opinion leaders.

The military had no time for self-professed heroes in the press. Ihsan Abd al-Quddus, a prominent journalist and later editor with the then-independent magazine *Rose al-Yusuf*, had acquired respect, clout, and a substantial readership during the brief transition period. One of the press's rising stars, he took the ultimate risk of "independently" reporting on the military. Following interviews with members of the RCC in an attempt to arrive at a common vision, ideology, perspective, philosophy, or worldview between them, he concluded with surprise that such a discordantly unimaginative group could not be described as anything but a gang. He ran the article under the title "The Gang that Rules Egypt." Abd al-Quddus thus crossed the red line and tested the military's limits. They felt inclined to act. Copies of *Rose al-Yusuf* were pulled off the stands with only a few thousand circulating. Abd al-Quddus was jailed for three months (and later pardoned). This incident would be the last time anyone from the press would break from the military's protocol.

For fifty-five years, the military has survived without having to give the media any unfettered access, let alone scrutiny. Any mention of the Egyptian Armed Forces in the media comes after a very rigid and paranoid vetting process and scrupulous attention to connotations. Interviews given to journalists by military officers were extremely infrequent and were limited to lofty, hyperbolic statements about its discipline, power, patriotism, and heroism. However, the level of secrecy at which the institution operated turned it into a black box for the media—a fourth branch of government, beyond transparency, accountability, or criticism. Insulated by layers of inaccessibility, the military was able to deflect attention from its growing assets in virtually every sector of Egyptian society—from the economy and politics to security, governance, and industry.

So when the uprising began in Egypt, the military was forced into the limelight, against its intention and better judgment. As the tanks and armored vehicles rolled into Tahrir Square on Friday, January 28 (known now as the Day of Rage), Egyptian protesters had no reason to believe that this was an adversarial posture. With no negative sentiments or even the mildest of criticism ever expressed in the state or private media in Egypt about the military, they were greeted as protectors of the public and impartial inter-mediaries in a standoff with the 'civilian regime' of the NDP. With little more than their vocal cords before a heavily armed force, protesters often chanted "the military and the people are one hand" whenever a face-off with the army seemed impending. The large number of protesters, their fervor, and their determination forced the military to avoid confrontation with them—a position the ruling military council would use as a rhetorical tool to convince the public that they were in fact the "guardians of the Revolution," despite their ardent attempts to empty Tahrir and curb further protests.

During the days that followed, some protesters began expressing skep-ticism about the military's so-called neutrality, which the evidence on the ground was beginning to contradict. For instance, on February 2, 2011, in the incident now infamously known as the "Battle of the Camel," videos collected by civilians and citizen journalists clearly show military vehicles clearing the way for armed Mubarak supporters on horse- and camelback as they descended onto Tahrir Square. Other videos collected by journalists documented visits by high-level military officials where they disparaged the protesters, questioned their motives, dismissed their concerns, and accused them of having destabilized the country. However, footage of this kind never ended up on the airwaves. With a media blackout on the mili-tary's cold stance vis-à-vis the protesters and a dramatic shift in the public discourse after the resignation of Mubarak, it was entirely unclear how this institution would affect things on the ground.

In his first major address, known as Bulletin Number 3, General Muhsin al-Fangari, a member of the Supreme Council of the Armed Forces (SCAF), in an attempt to sound strong-willed and decisive, ended up over-stating his case, suggesting hesitance and lack of confidence. Stuttering in an uncomposed fashion, not only does al-Fangari commend and thank President Mubarak for his thirty years of service to the country, he offers the martyrs of the revolution a reassuring military salute. It was evident at this point that he had not received any media training and that the armed forces were not ready for prime time just yet. The unseasoned nature of this first address signified a sentiment of comfort among Egyptians who trusted that the military would defend the revolution's goals and see it through to fruition. This framing of the military's position in revolution-ary terms was intended to signify a commitment by the military to the revolution and the memory of the fallen. Since this brief and encouraging statement, SCAF has employed a multi-pronged and shifting strategy in its relationship with the media in the country.

This was the opening salvo in what was to be become a turbulent relationship between SCAF and the media over the next ten months. Al-Fangari would become famous for a SCAF public statement he gave on July 12, 2011 in which he spoke in an ominous, Darth Vader–like tone that exuded power and resolve, to either intimidate, frighten, or calm those looking for comfort in safety. Most notable about the speech was its peculiar delivery. The general projected and changed the tone of his voice in an awkward manner that suggested either nervousness or inexperience. But the notoriety al-Fangari (whose name in Arabic sounds like the English word 'finger') acquired was a result of his seemingly reprimanding and threatening finger-waving throughout the speech. Since this speech, several Facebook groups were created in response, the most popular being "Fangari, You Cannot Threaten Us."

Throughout the first year after the toppling of Mubarak, SCAF focused on celebrations of military accomplishments and success, and deflected attention away from the celebration of the uprising. These included three festivities, one on the anniversary of the July 23, 1952 coup d'état and twice to celebrate the October 1973 War against Israel, once on the Gregorian calendar date of October 6 and again on its Hijri date of 10 Ramadan, with SCAF head Muhammad Husayn Tantawi making public statements on both occasions.

SCAF has had a short but extremely eventful time in power following Mubarak's fall. While the council rose out of the remains of the Mubarak government—each of the nineteen members served under his rule and benefited greatly from their loyalty to the regime—they have nevertheless attempted to rebrand the council as an independent institution with no links to the NDP bureaucracy. Since I will be unable to cover the structure, politics, management, and economic viability of military power in Egypt in any depth here, my intention instead is to examine the manner in which the country's executive board and surrogate president addresses, curbs, manages, cajoles, and responds to the media.

They had accepted the need for the state and private media to criticize the old regime, but they wished to maintain the immunity of the military from such scrutiny. To their advantage, there was already a legal doctrine in place to insulate them from public criticism. This is Law No. 313 of 1956, passed as a presidential decree and amended in 1967, which heavily restricts coverage of the military. The law reads as follows:

This decree prohibits publishing or broadcasting any information or news on the armed forces and its formations, movements, equipment, and personnel. In other words, all matters related to strategic and military aspects cannot be published or broadcast by any means without obtaining the written consent of the director of military intelligence, or his deputy in his absence. The decree also identifies the penalty for violating its provisions.

In the first case of its kind since SCAF took over, a military court sentenced blogger Maikel Nabil to five years in jail in a swift tribunal for criticizing the military in his blog post entitled "The Military and the People Are Not One Hand." Under such conditions, and with SCAF formally administering the country, it would have been practically impossible to meet the demands of the decree, as the military now had a hand in every aspect of governance. But the existence of the law resulted in a significant reluctance by the media to discuss matters related to the military. Instead, the private media sought commentary from the military regarding various developments on political, economic, security, and social matters. The first few months of SCAF rule can be characterized as a period of media shyness. Officials and members of SCAF were very reluctant to go on air; many avoided interviews, and preferred private conversations with television producers and journalists over formal interviews. Statements could not be released without permission from superiors, and, given the growing burden on SCAF, there was a genuine concern that messages would not corroborate one another. Instead, the military attempted to position itself in relation to the inner circuit of the private media professionals, to befriend them, to build rapport, and to offer support to ensure favorable treatment. This was a rather successful period for the military, as confrontations with protester demands had not reached a high point and they were able to maintain a low profile, thereby using the interim government as a scapegoat.

When it became evident by the summer of 2011 that little progress had been made on many fronts, from continued military trials of civilians to the reluctance to try Mubarak and other NDP officials for crimes committed during the January uprising, the media sensed that the government of prime minister Essam Sharaf was actually incapable of addressing any concerns and may not have had the authority to act on the demands of the revolution. This was when the military became the subject of much curiosity and inquiry by journalists and reporters. Additionally, questionable actions by the military became more frequent with little redress, raising more questions about their conduct and putting more pressure on the media to pose penetrating questions.

The performance of SCAF and its media arm during the first year of the transition, with all of its blunders between February 11, 2011 and January 23, 2012—including the Maspero attacks, the Balloon Theater incident (which led to clashes between the families of the uprisings' victims and the police), both of the Muhammad Mahmud battles, the Cabinet sit-in battles, and several rounds of confrontation in Abbasiya—was totally catastrophic. Not only was the cost in lives in the hundreds and injuries in the thousands, but with every public statement from SCAF, their image in front of the public was deteriorating swiftly. By dismissing observable realities documented extensively through videographic evidence, SCAF's press conferences looked amateurish, one-sided, and overly scripted and rehearsed. Their believability lessened with each incident. This was akin to an ostrich burying its head in the sand to avoid the public wrath.

Yet a crucial turning point for SCAF's public image came after the swearing-in of the newly elected parliament on January 23, 2012. On this date, with the parliament garnering all the attention, especially its surprising composition of 75 percent Islamist, much of the limelight was drawn away from the ruling council. Around the same time, public criticism of SCAF began to drop drastically as the attention of both the media and the public was diverted to the elected body. Even SCAF-related hashtags on Twitter dropped significantly. The ostrich had gone from having its head in the sand to camouflaging its body as well. This was confirmed on January 31, 2012, when it was announced that General Ismail Etman, SCAF member and head of morale affairs in the military (a task that makes him the chief intermediary with the media), was relieved of his job in a public statement that claimed he had reached retirement age. Despite this, in the following days Etman appeared to continue serving as a SCAF spokesperson to the media, giving several interviews and releasing statements on the Port Said massacre and the ensuing violence. But this was the beginning of a phasing out of SCAF media presence.

Prior to the public disappearance of SCAF from the public eye, Field Marshal Muhammad Husayn Tantawi had always maintained a very low profile, with other members of the council given permission to communicate on behalf of the armed forces on Egyptian state and private media. On the government networks, their interviews went smoothly and without tumult. On the private networks, they were met with difficult questions that they often either overreacted to, dismissed entirely, or answered clumsily. Examples of media blunders abound, including one program where SCAF member Hasan al-Ruwayni accidentally admitted on a private network that he was responsible for spreading rumors during the eighteen-day protest in January and February to encourage demonstrators to leave Tahrir. On another occasion, SCAF member General Mamduh Shahin gave conflicting accounts of the constitutional principles and the conduct of elections for different channels and at different times. These interviews exposed SCAF as an institution incapable of asserting a clear, unequivocal message and ill equipped to handle a free and independent media environment. This was extremely obvious when two SCAF members gave a lengthy interview following the Maspero clashes in mid-October in which they were hardly capable of deflecting criticism.

The head of SCAF, Tantawi, has been camera-shy throughout. He has only given three speeches since assuming leadership of the country. Other videos are very carefully chosen and are often orchestrated. One video released some months ago shows him in civilian clothes walking in downtown Cairo and being greeted by passersby; it was meant to illustrate his popularity and accessibility. The other two were taken at various ceremonies and events, each showing him speaking candidly about the state of the country and calling for an end to protests, sit-ins, strikes, and other acts of civil disobedience. The clumsiness of these videos is evident from their inability to present him as a coherent interlocutor. In one of them, a SCAF member and the chief of staff for the armed forces, Sami Anan, is seen dictating to Tantawi and completing his sentences for him. In another video, Tantawi is visibly hesitant and inarticulate. And in yet another video, dated October 2, he is seen as a more authoritative figure verbally reprimanding any Egyptians who continue "destabilizing" the country with protests. He speaks to his subordinates with a paternalistic voice, turning often to then-prime minister Essam Sharaf, whose head hangs in a dejected fashion as he stares at the ground. When Tantawi asks Sharaf if he agrees with him, Sharaf responds compliantly with nods of the head. On many other occasions, other members of SCAF are given the job of addressing the media.

Few members of SCAF seem to have survived the barrage of criticism for media incompetency. The most notable of the few is the second in command after Tantawi, General Sami Anan. By avoiding the media entirely and serving only as an interlocutor on behalf of the field marshal in meetings with political actors and public opinion heavyweights, he has effectively avoided any scrutiny and remains a mirage, beyond incrimination. He has no faults on the record and is walking away from the transition with a seemingly pristine slate, which may position him not only to survive the transition, but to withstand any calls for justice against SCAF in the immediate or long-term future. With Tantawi at the center of most SCAF criticism, in addition to his disappointing public displays, his long tenure under Mubarak, and his advanced age, Sami Anan's media invisibility may be serving him well as the man-in-waiting.

In many instances, their interactions with reporters and journalists angered the media professionals because they were expected to comply with the military's rules when that was considered unacceptable journalistically. There are plenty of accounts and testimonies from journalists regarding inappropriate correspondences or phone calls from military agencies with differing tones, from appeasement to veiled threats. As time has gone on, SCAF has gone from using the carrot to win over the private media to the stick in attempts to discourage them from their investigations.

As the conflict between the protest movements and SCAF escalated, so did the military's desire to control negative messages broadcast locally, regionally, and internationally. This means that in cases where there is significant violence and loss of life (a frequent occurrence since September 2011) involving the military, SCAF turns from benevolent to malevolent. In such cases, SCAF often publicly criticizes the private media, and holds press conferences where all accusations against them are completely dismissed, even in the presence of credible photographic and videographic evidence.

On December 17, SCAF entered a new era in its media messaging—the online-video/citizen-journalism realm. There is evidence that the military had infiltrated the protester campsites and collected content. In many instances, plainclothes military recruits were sent into the protesters' ranks to shoot footage that could then be used to incriminate them. This video was disseminated widely online and sent to the television networks for broadcast to counter "propaganda" against the military. The state media presented it as fact, while most private media subjected it to close examination and scrutiny.

This 'head in the sand' technique, akin to Mubarak's approach for at least a decade, has so far served SCAF well as they capitalize on growing public distress over unrest in the country. They have also effectively desensitized the Egyptian public against violence committed against protesters by the military. While in the summer of 2010 there was public outrage at the death of Khaled Said at the hands of the police simply through the image of his contorted face, today the near-weekly gruesome photos and videos of protesters killed with live ammunition, crushed under military vehicles, stripped and beaten, and sexually violated women are numerous enough that the public threshold for outrage has increased dramatically. Coupled with what looks to the average Egyptian like a military shepherding the country toward free elections and democratic civilian rule, the demands of the protesters, although legitimate, have become far less sustainable in the eyes of the majority of Egyptians.

Hence, SCAF has effectively created a great deal of discord between political parties, movements, youth, and revolutionaries, effectively demoralizing the public about the revolution. In the end, the Egyptian public may very well accept military rule in the face of what looks like protest-sponsored chaos. Yet SCAF's greatest hurdle—besides a growing social justice–oriented protest movement in factories, industries, and labor groups and syndicates—remains the private media, who have yet to relent under the growing pressure to accept the military's directives. In one decree, newspapers that were licensed before the law were asked to reapply in the Morale Affairs Directorate of the military and obtain new approval. Furthermore, all topics, news, statements, complaints, advertisements, and photographs pertaining to the armed forces must be approved before publication. The Committee to Protect Journalists described it as the single most serious setback to the freedom of the press since the fall of Mubarak. Few publications complied. A military censor for the press was appointed, and many columnists responded disparagingly. Some independent newspapers have violated the censorship requirement entirely, thereby blatantly calling SCAF's bluff and taunting the military to take action against them.

The latest phenomenon is the growing cult of expertise. SCAF deploys what are now called 'strategic experts'—members of the military who come to the defense of SCAF publicly. They attempt to distance and insulate SCAF from criticism, after consecutive failures of the council to explain itself on the air. They try to sound impartial and objective as professionals. The 'strategic experts' create a buffer, so that if they fail to communicate convincingly, or in the event of confrontation or scandalous gaffes, the outcomes do not backfire on SCAF. A good example of this is General Abd al-Mun'im Kato's now infamous interview with *al-Sharq al-Awsat* regarding the military's treatment of protesters. When General Kato spoke to the media, he was speaking from a position of close proximity to SCAF, and the council encouraged him to be an interlocutor for the military. This is not a haphazard process. The military is extremely cautious and paranoid about who represents it. Kato began communicating on behalf of the military as early as January 28, 2011, when he encouraged protesters to return to their homes. At no point was he considered persona non grata until he stumbled publicly, whereupon SCAF abandoned him as a spokesperson and openly denied any affiliation with him. Even SCAF's representative in the United States, General Muhammad Kishki, declared that General Kato did not represent SCAF in any way or at any time.

Both SCAF and the government have made marked progress in this online arena. Both have adopted social media to relay announcements and to gauge public opinion in the form of polls, press releases, bulletins, and experimental decrees. In many instances, SCAF has released announcements on its Facebook page before delivery to the state media. Most recently, in the clashes with protesters at the Cabinet buildings, SCAF has even released edited videos of the clashes taken from among the ranks of civilians that they claim were protesters. So the military has itself recruited 'amateur military journalist' brigades and social media teams to counter online activists.

When the Facebook page first appeared, most of the comments on it were very complimentary of the military and there was genuine fear that any contrarian message would pose a threat to whoever posted it. As SCAF's popularity waned (especially within Egypt's cyber-community) due to consecutive acts of mismanagement and miscommunication, more critical voices have used the page to express their anger, frustration, and disdain for the military's actions. This is a marked transformation in the page's traffic. Much like SCAF's traditional media approach, which focuses on misdirection and ignoring criticism, the Facebook page also rarely engages with critics. Instead, postings are confined to bulletins from the highest ranks of SCAF. The absence of any nimbleness and the seemingly hierarchical approach to information dissemination, forcing every expression to be vetted by the higher ranks, has left the page woefully anachronistic and out of touch with contemporary online discourses. Furthermore, its use of classical Arabic, compared to the colloquial and slang Egyptian dialect on many activist pages, has made it uninviting and extremely old-fashioned. Yet SCAF seems to have successfully recruited developers and supporters using the Facebook page, as described by one of the administrators in a status posting.

Despite this, SCAF's greatest challenge both online and offline came courtesy of an activist campaign known as Kazibun, whose objective was to transmit evidence against SCAF from the online social-media echo chamber to the 75 percent of Egyptians who do not use the Internet. On hundreds of occasions, activists and volunteers took videos gathered by citizen journalists and protesters depicting violence committed by the military and held flash mob–style street screenings using mobile projectors in heavy traffic areas in Cairo and Alexandria. On at least a handful of occasions they were met with violence by SCAF supporters, both organized and spontaneous. In every such incident of attack (in most instances, these are attacks against the equipment rather than persons), the commotion drew more attention to the Kazibun campaign and turned the settings into impromptu anti-SCAF rallies. For this reason, it was important for SCAF to go from denying the accusations of violence to disappearing completely.

The commencement of the parliament's operations in January 2012 ushered in another period in SCAF's management of their public image during the transition. The ruling council had effectively disappeared from the public eye. More reluctant than ever to make public statements and avoiding the limelight at all cost, they were able to deflect attention from the interim government on issues of mismanagement and violations by the security apparatus, thereby insulating themselves from public criticism. Simultaneously, the parliament, dominated by the Islamist camps of the Freedom and Justice Party (FJP) and the al-Nour Party, turned into an arena for cacophonous deliberation and combative interaction. The spectacle of discord and competition in the parliament shifted the public eye away from the government and SCAF and toward the elected body in an attempt to conceal what had quickly begun looking like a junta unable to manage the country. Furthermore, there seemed to be a genuine effort to resuscitate in Egypt a 'deep state' that is insulated from public purview and admonishment. The parliament's extremely explosive sessions in its first few weeks illustrated the growing polarization between political forces critical of SCAF and those who are willing to excuse them.

In sum, SCAF began its tenure with significant tremors as they improvised their way through the first few months, slowly discovering their weakness in utilizing the media and working toward rectifying this. Rather than investing in improving their public image, however, SCAF expedited their public disappearance. It should be no surprise to anyone if the ruling military council orchestrated a weakened presidency, a crippled parliament, and a loyal judiciary, all of which can serve as the façade of legitimacy concealing the same military power that has ruled the country since 1952, resealing Pandora's box.

A Seven A

July 14, 2012

hen comedian Ahmed Mekky uttered the Latinized acronym
"A-7-A" in his film *H Dabbour*, he broke a taboo in the film
industry. But because he spelled it out in English, its incom-
prehensibility to the censors and anyone with little online knowledge
allowed it to slip through the ironclad grip of Mubarak-era cinema gate-
keepers. *Aha*, the slang colloquial Egyptian word (also used in some areas
of the Levant) has no specific meaning but is commonly used in versatile
contexts not unlike the English exclamation "Fuck!" Yet the term, whose
etymological roots are very difficult to disentangle, remains a salient part
of Egyptians' expression of disdain, shock, agony, anger, and a plethora of
other hyperbolic emotional states. Whether it is a verb, noun, adjective, or
onomatopoeia is inconsequential, as its meaning is understood. In a personal conversation with writer and blogger Ahmad Nagi in February 2008,
he lashed out against the culture of conformity and the high premium paid
to those who speak in polite euphemisms about the state of their lives and
country. "So what if I say *a7a*! It is how we speak in this country! We hide
behind politeness and accept what is happening around us!"

The term is not a newcomer to the Egyptian vernacular. Anecdote and
testimony suggest that the masses pleading with Nasser not to abdicate
after the humiliating defeat of 1967 shouted "*A7a, a7a, la tatanaha!*" (A7a,
a7a, don't abdicate!). Since the revolution, it has been used publicly to
reflect on the deterioration of the country's political arena, from songs
like "*A7a ya thawra*" by Ahmad al-Sawi to songs by the Ultras.

However, its frequency in Egyptian speech underscores an explosion of
public expression that is unadulterated and unhindered. Historically, the
fissures between socioeconomic classes in the country were maintained

not only by access to authority and power but also through the admonishment of the masses, on the grounds of what is often described as 'vulgarity' or its Arabic equivalent *bi'a* (which literally means 'environment' but is the mid-1980s abbreviation of the expression *bi'a masriya wiskha*, or 'dirty Egyptian environment'). This widely used category of disparagement and condescension is leveled at those whose behavior is deemed unbecoming, by asserting hierarchy and class and creating divisions in terms of social standards as well as access to resources. It is deployed with incredible frequency to describe Egyptians who bring pots of cooked food to the beach (because not everyone can afford exorbitant seaside services), people who speak at a higher decibel level, and almost certainly toward individuals who use profanities to express their anguish. To Egypt's elite, there are the polite, respectful needy and there are the *bi'a*, undignified poor. *A7a* is the explosive, screeching, unnerving, alarming, and deafening yell of the latter.

In a country whose masses are economically depressed, sexually repressed, politically suppressed, and socially distressed, *a7a* is the semiotic sum of all dissident expression against the tyranny of the status quo. And as class consciousness shakes to its core under the feet of a mass revolutionary movement, so has its vernacular. *A7a* now permeates all social classes with fervor, shattering social norms and elite mores. Both the enfranchised and the disenfranchised turn to it in frustration and camaraderie, even under the nose of societal etiquette and the dominion of all authorities (whether armed with bullets, ideology, or purported holiness). At a time when the state's role was to avoid at all costs *khadsh haya'* (scratching the modesty) of society—a precursor to the collapse of political honor—Egyptians, literary and lay, have empowered vulgarity and turned it into an arena for awe-inspiring creativity and a space for aesthetic brilliance. One example is the independent yet immensely popular song "*A7a al-shibshib daa*" (A7a, the slipper is lost). The expletive-packed track that went viral online is part of a growing synthesizer-rich genre of Egyptian folkloric music pioneered by the young artists Oka and Ortega that irreverently uses slang terms and working-class expressions to narrate experience. Despite its popularity, "*A7a al-shibshib daa*" has never aired on any radio station or featured on any television program, not even to discuss it as a phenomenon. Such is the extent of its violation of public morality and cultural decorum. Nevertheless, its immense appeal is an indication of the growing popular acceptance of such violation.

Yet the revolutionary artists, writers, musicians, and activists of this period are walking in the footsteps of generations of their predecessors, who rescued expression and language from the fangs of power for many years. Dating as far back as 1150 BC, ancient Egyptian artists produced what are now known as the satirical and erotic papyri, which ridiculed the pharaohs and royalty by depicting them as animals doing frivolous things in the face of that period's culture of megalomaniacal self-deification. In other images, scruffy, balding, and overweight men with comically oversized genitalia are shown performing sexual acts with many women in a fantastical fashion. Such images are a direct challenge to the absolute virility of the omnipotent god-kings. And the story continues. From Naguib Surur's infamous series of poems *Kussummiyat* (a long multi-part poem representing an enraged tirade about the state of Egypt and its people), which was banned from circulation in Egypt for decades, to Khairy Shalaby's extraordinarily explicit and evocative novels, such as *Wikalat 'Atiya* (translated as *The Lodging House*) about the lives of people in Cairo's *ashwa'iyat* (urban slums), Egypt's creative class has all too often used profanity to amplify the pulse of the street to the ivory towers.

Wikalat 'Atiya's protagonist, who becomes a dweller in the impoverished shantytown, witnesses livelihoods on the fringes of social acceptability. A novel teeming with colloquial epithets, it goes further than most modern works by describing social anomaly with remarkable vividness, including such characters as Demiana, the monkey keeper who engages in a sadistic and exploitative sexual relationship with her eldest primate. And while this story may seem entirely apolitical, Shalaby's stubborn intent to position the fringe squarely at the center of his seventy works is itself a political confrontation with the regime even when the regime fails to acknowledge it. The late Surur's *Kussummiyat* probably goes farthest in its damning lament of Egypt's state in the wake of the 1967 defeat. He recites at one point, "It is not rude to say '*kussummiyat*' [mothers' pussies] when I am fucked, there is no more honor, modesty, fault, or crap. Egypt is before my eyes with its pussy stuffed from all the fucking, full of abscesses, and we are without resort." With similar sarcastic caricature in April 2008, during an interview with Al Jazeera, the dissident poet Ahmad Fouad Negm recited a new poem alluding to Gamal Mubarak called *Aris al-dawla* (The State's Groom), saying, "Exit one heaven and enter another, it makes no difference to us. It does no injury to our bodies, it doesn't break our hearts or bust our balls," before the interview was swiftly cut short. And while the Mubarak regime felt that a good joke is just that, a joke, the cacophony of jokes eventually grew too loud.

Today no one is above the ridicule and sharp-tongued criticism of a newly liberated Egyptian public. In one spoof music video posted on the expletive-ridden YouTube comedy channel Bahgaga, President Morsi is sung to by a bikini-clad woman who repeatedly lifts her top in an attempt to conceal her nipples from broad daylight. Other works by the same channel include voiceovers from parliamentary sessions where elected members discuss the police's use of birdshot in the faces of protesters, using gratuitous references to human anatomy. Another video voiceover depicts a parliamentary discussion where house speaker Sa'd al-Katatni and top delegates of the Muslim Brotherhood visit Saudi Arabia to defuse a recent public spat. One of the members accuses the visitors of not only performing fellatio on the king but also allowing him to mount them as a sign of complete submission, all of this described in the most distressingly detailed and explicit language. And in a sign of Egyptian society's complete irreverence even toward the Custodian of the Two Holy Mosques, King Abdullah, the monarch has been depicted recently by Cairene graffiti artist Keizer in a caricature with the inscription "Your Majesty's ass is red." Even Islamist political platforms are not immune from profane public criticism, including a widely circulated voiceover of an al-Nour party commercial suggesting the protagonist is a sex-crazed pedophile.

Hence the threat to power comes not from political adversaries alone but from the same creative class that produced the *sa'aliq* (vagabonds) of yesteryear, people like poet Abd al-Hamid al-Dib, writer Mahmud al-Sa'dany, and others. Al-Dib, often referred to as *al-sha'ir al-sa'luq* (the vagabond poet), lived a life of perpetual poverty and dissent, writing poetry and reciting a large amount of unpublished Egyptian colloquial poetry that would otherwise be publicly unacceptable, such as the poem "Kuss umm al-dahr al-ahmar" (Fuck the Red Destiny). Many of the lives of such *sa'aliq* are documented in the beautifully written, nostalgic account of the late chronicler Yousef al-Sherif.

With a third of Egyptians now online, much of the language deemed unacceptable in public is flourishing online as the latitude of linguistic norms is infinitely wider. Blogger Wael Abbas has garnered more followers and adversaries recently due to his generous use of offensive sexual references. Discussion forums online, as well as comment threads on news sites, have become a platform for competitive offensive barbs and slang sparring matches featuring the most disruptive and offensive language possible. The obliteration of any social or public tact, and of the very notion of acceptability in these spaces, renders them liberating. In fact, this is so much the case that even the administrators of the media sites struggle to contain the all-too-frequent cascades of insults and counter-insults.

As President Morsi trades jabs with SCAF and the judiciary over the legality of the elected parliament, high-level insult is not uncommon; all sides rally supporters from the ranks of the public to strengthen their ranks. Neither Field Marshal Tantawi, nor the Supreme Guide of the Muslim Brotherhood Muhammad Badi‘, nor Shaykh of al-Azhar Ahmad al-Tayyib, nor any other revered individual or office is above being targeted by the unrelenting whips of public tongues. In our days of political jockeying, uncertainty, and disparagement, many are resorting to the versatile three-letter word *aja*—for refuge, release, and revolt.

Patron Saints

July 23, 2012

E gypt's revolution was leaderless by design and not happenstance—
by will and not circumstance. But not everyone got the memo.
Today, legions gravitate toward one notable or another, one
visionary or another, one shaykh or another, one demagogue or another.
Today there are those who describe themselves as "Hazimun," the fol-
lowers of Shaykh Hazim Abu Ismail, or those who consider themselves
ElBaradei's Ultras. There are those who see the Brotherhood's Supreme
Guide as clairvoyant and those who mourned for months the death of
Pope Shenouda as if a connection to God had been permanently severed.
Some flock after Shaykh Wagdi Ghonim's fiery vitriol and others watch
hours of inflammatory online videos of the defrocked and exiled Father
Zakariya Botros. In the end, there's plenty of hand-kissing going on these
days, and in almost dizzying fashion. At a time when Egyptian institutions
are fighting for their survival, and as the country slowly becomes a ter-
rain of self-rule, celebrity messiahs, saviors, and deliverers are a pound a
dozen. They are auxiliary instruments whose seemingly rogue contrarian
posturing does little beyond nudge age-old institutions toward greater
hegemony over society.

All institutions have inherent problems, which are magnified and
aggravated within religious institutions specifically. They are hierarchical
structures that emphasize conformity, render their subjects dependent,
and enshrine a chain of command. Their process of specialization in their
ranks leads to ultraspecialization and the disappearance of peripheral vision.
Designed to increase efficiency and improve transfer of talent, information,
and resources, they are instead killing the spirit of inquisitiveness, destroying intellectual curiosity, and digging a grave for Egypt's polymaths.

Take for instance, al-Azhar, which without any doubt is an institution of remarkable repute and international acclaim, and one of the oldest academies in the world. Over the past sixty years, it has slowly relinquished its independence and become subservient to the state. With al-Azhar's work limited to reaffirming the priorities of the sitting government, the state's hegemony over it ensured that its supervision of religious jurisprudence was either severely hindered or harmonious with the state's intentions.

Not long ago, an education at al-Azhar was the most sought-after by sons of the working class in the country's rural governorates. Because of the prestige of Azhari education in rural Egypt, hundreds of thousands flocked to Cairo over the past three generations to be trained in religious affairs and then to return to respectable jobs in their hometowns. Simultaneously, over the past few decades and on very much the same grounds in the country's towns and villages, the Muslim Brotherhood developed its confessional and doctrinal platforms in the political, economic, and social realms, expanding its reach almost in parallel to al-Azhar.

The two have avoided confrontation, at least overtly, for much of the past few decades, with only occasional spats between the Supreme Guide of the Brotherhood and the Shaykh of al-Azhar. Neither was prepared to throw the other under the bus, but both understood that they were on overlapping territory. Despite supporting their political adversaries, al-Azhar avoided incriminating the Brotherhood entirely (although the religious institution merely stood by as former regimes punished them). In return, the Brotherhood consciously decided not to undermine al-Azhar in their working-class strongholds.

The January 25 uprising and the ensuing turmoil have left al-Azhar utterly disoriented. With their ability to control their own institution hindered, Azharis have splintered, with elements supporting the Brotherhood, with groups critical of both the Brotherhood and the Salafis, and with yet other groups siding with the amorphous leftist nationalist revolutionary fronts. With al-Azhar incapable of pulling its rank, the Brotherhood and Salafi groups filled the void by taking advantage of the institution's delayed and reluctant public statements and dwindling reach. Today, as if in punishment for their former collusion with the Mubarak regime, al-Azhar has been marginalized by the Brotherhood. Nowhere was this more glaring and startling than when the shaykh of al-Azhar was seated at the back of an auditorium for President Morsi's speech at Cairo University before his swearing-in. Al-Azhar's proud pontiff stormed out in defiance and displeasure.

Even in the constitutional assembly, Islamist operators negotiating with SCAF and other political groups insisted that al-Azhar's designated seats be considered among those of civil society, not the Islamist current. So the marginalization of al-Azhar has become systematic, perhaps with the positive effect of deinstitutionalizing its revered stature or demystifying religion, perhaps making it more egalitarian, or maybe shattering the blind acceptance that is so obdurate within it. However, there is every indication that whatever might replace al-Azhar's religious reach will emulate its most undesirable qualities and ignore its most commendable. The Muslim Brotherhood and the Salafi groups are likely to reproduce its hierarchy, already evident in their preexisting structure, while hastily and clumsily dismissing al-Azhar's most redeeming quality: careful and studious scholarship on matters of faith and practice.

As for the Church, al-Azhar's twin, there is no questioning that the institution is now reaping the harvest of its most misguided, albeit well-intentioned, decisions and actions over the past few decades. Although its history of nationalistic commitment is luminous, it has engineered, largely out of fear and clientelism, a near-absolute annexation of all aspects of private and public life for Egypt's Copts. With Sadat's abrupt breaking of the social contract between the state and Christians, the Church assumed complete guardianship over the Coptic flock, from feeding them and employing them to the provision of services. Beyond the Church's original task of spiritual guidance, it subsumed everything from their children's sporting activities to their secular celebrations.

This was all done with the state's support and guidance. In the end, as far as Mubarak was concerned, there was no Coptic matter that could not be resolved by a single phone call to a single Copt—Pope Shenouda. So the state guaranteed Christians complete safety from the propped-up perennial ghost, the Brotherhood, in exchange for unequivocal silence and blind obedience. This could only be delivered if the Church had full and unchallenged control over its flock, both politically and socially. And the Church succeeded, and delivered precisely that.

Today, the times are changing as the Church finds itself in the same predicament as al-Azhar. It is literally bursting at the seams. While some Christians are fearful of the days ahead, seizing any means of escape from the country, the vast majority are here to stay. They are vocally and actively participating in all aspects of public life. No longer passively agreeing that the Church should represent their political will or best interests, they are no longer a unified front. Instead they act and engage as citizens. Their visibility is also at an all-time high.

Nevertheless, through its Millet Council and governance bodies, the Church remains forceful in its intent to speak for the country's religious minority, something many Copts refuse. This was most evident when the late Pope Shenouda was forgivingly hosting SCAF's generals after the October 9, 2011 massacre, while the Maspero Youth Union chanted against them. For much of the last eighteen months, the Church has tried every tool at its disposal to bring such groups under its wing, but to no avail. The patriarchate, like al-Azhar, is at a crossroads. Seeking refuge with the military or siding with the Muslim Brotherhood—neither scenario is favorable. In the end, and despite the turbulence, al-Azhar and the Church will outlive this episode, each relying on its legacy, authority, and constituency. Al-Azhar will likely end up with the constitutionally sanctioned last say on all *sharia*-related matters and the Church will continue to preside over Christian affairs.

The irony is that, without exception, all parties in this game of constitutional and political musical chairs (SCAF, the Muslim Brotherhood, Salafis, al-Azhar, the Church) are embodiments of counterrevolution, in their classist schisms, rigid hierarchy, deification of authority, commitment to neoliberal economics, and admonishment of internal dissonance. Assuming all religious institutions are well-meaning and benevolent, we still see how their love, affection, and care for their subjects have turned tutorship into sponsorship, protection into oppression, and guardianship into custody. For this reason, the late activist Mina Danial and Azhari shaykh Emad Effat, both killed while disobeying draconian decrees to avoid revolutionary struggle, represent critical dissenting currents. While al-Azhar, the Church, the Brotherhood, and·other deep organizations have much to learn from their margins, there are few indications that this is happening. It is not in the nature of paternalistic institutions to willfully forgo saintly patronage over "their" masses.

Tragedy and Farce

August 7, 2012

In a span of ten days, Palestinians killed sixteen Egyptian guards near the border in their fight against Israel, Amr al-Bunni committed suicide by trying to collect his wages from Nile City Towers, and Mo'az Muhammad lost his life to a burnt shirt in Dahshur. In Egypt today, tragedy and farce are two faces of the same coin.

Intertwined within each of these deaths are layers of tragedy and decades of injustice. Yet all of this is lost in the noise of polarized perspectives and historic amnesia. So when Egyptian soldiers on duty near the Rafah border were attacked and killed in a shadowy suspicious incident where the objectives of the assailants seem largely beyond logical comprehension, the distribution of blame was weighted in favor of the farcical. Surely the Palestinian militants acted against their own interests by attacking their allies and jeopardizing relations with Egypt, losing the sympathy of Egyptians, and blockading themselves as the border shut. Even under Mubarak, arguably the most hostile Egyptian regime to the well-being of Palestinians in Gaza, no attack of this sort or scale had ever occurred, let alone during a time when Hamas leader and prime minister Ismail Haniyeh is received in a ceremony befitting a president of Palestine by Muhammad Morsi. Children and teenagers stood on either side of the road carrying Hamas and Muslim Brotherhood flags as the vehicle procession drove by.

And if it is not the Palestinians, then it must certainly be Sinai's Bedouins whose "unfounded" anger, frustration, and animosity toward the Egyptian state may have caused them to commit such a crime. What do they have to complain about besides having their land annexed by the state, sold at comical prices to investors and developers, and then locked out of employment and revenue-generating possibilities for two decades?

Are they not content with their lives becoming global clichés, as tourists dress in their likeness and go on desert excursions to drink coffee under the stars to appreciate their prehistoric lifestyles? Surely they understand that the years of frequent and systematic arrest, interrogation, and mistreatment of their kin are imperative in the name of national security.

And when cars burned outside the Nile City Towers, a long list of explanations was offered except the one that is clear as day—the crude and dehumanizing juxtaposition of absolute wealth with abject poverty and the exploitation of the latter. Fundamentally, Amr al-Bunni was killed by greed. The question is: Which greed do you wish to blame? Al-Bunni's for demanding his meager pay for temporary security work? Or that of a multibillion-pound high-rise management/ownership prepared to terminate a life to protect its assets? Yet the farce comes with at least a pinch of irony. When al-Bunni forcefully demanded what was rightfully his, he immediately metamorphosed from hero to villain, protector to threat, guard to *baltagi*.

In Dahshur, clashes erupted between Christians and Muslims. The spectacle of an over-ironed shirt highlighted the fragility of the country's interreligious harmony and exposed a system that absolves rather than resolves. With Christian businesses and homes attacked as retribution for both the damaged shirt and the death of Mo'az Muhammad, the state has done nothing but postpone reconciliation, perhaps to reap the tragedy tenfold in the future. And for an elitist media whose condescension toward the masses is jarring, the problem is again all about the ignorant radical poor— so much so that as I watched one talk-show host discuss the incident, I expected him to half-jokingly suggest the government issue spanking new irons to Christian laundry owners to avert such occurrences in the future!

Egypt this past week reminds me of George Orwell's somewhat autobiographical 1936 short story "Shooting an Elephant," which describes the dilemma of a young British colonial officer in Burma named Moulmein when an elephant went rogue and ravaged a village where he was stationed. In a fit of rage, the elephant brutalized homes and stomped a man, spreading fear and fury among the villagers. They turned to Moulmein as the only person with a rifle, but by the time he reached the scene, the colossal creature had become tranquil again, calmly meandering and grazing. Despised by the villagers for representing the crown and its exploitation of the locals, Moulmein desperately wanted to win them over. But by killing a work elephant, he would be ending a life, destroying a piece of "working machinery," and impoverishing its owner. Despite the fact that the danger had passed, the pressure from the angry villagers continued to mount around him. They wanted that elephant dead. With the burden of centuries of colonial enterprise on his shoulders and a deep visceral desire to be chummy with the ruled, he shot the elephant.

Just as Moulmein's shooting of the elephant failed to save the British imperial project from its inevitable demise, the 'combing' of Sinai will not uproot threats to state integrity, the securing of Dahshur will not mend a shirt or the long-term wounds, and the barricading of Nile City Towers will not conceal the desperation that surrounds the shimmering towers. But for now at least, farce triumphs over tragedy.

The State of Anarchy

August 10, 2012

gyptian politicians, legislators, military men, clergy, entrepreneurs, and lawyers are now at each others' throats over their access to the country's higher state institutions, the privileges associated with these, and access to the things that make the country tick. What most of these groups don't realize is that they are splitting a pie that has already been eaten. They are fighting over property that doesn't exist. They're trying to bottle water from a mirage. The Egyptian state has already fallen.

Its collapse had been impending for much of the last decade. With the social contract between Mubarak's regime and the public at large effectively severed, and with aggressive neoliberalization policies impoverishing all but a small sliver of the Egyptian populace, self-sufficiency, *fahlawa* (street smarts), charity, improvisation, and good fortune are the factors preventing the country from becoming a failed state. In the last decade, the Mubarak regime has decimated food subsidies, destroyed the public education system, laid waste to the public healthcare system, done little to address rising unemployment, and effectively stopped functioning as a state. So out of touch was this shell of a state that it continued to implore and coerce the penniless masses to pay their taxes (out of discipline and behavioral regimenting and conditioning) while relieving those who can afford it. So Egyptians did what they usually do in such circumstances—they didn't pay. The same happened with licenses, traffic tickets, school fees, food, and supplies of all kinds.

It seemed every Egyptian short of the professional class and the bourgeoisie elite were engaged in *talqit rizk* ('collecting their portions' or 'making ends meet'). Much of the country seemed to work around the rules through *wasta* (connections), a small tip, a little charm, and/ or humor. Things in Egypt have a way of working even in the direst of circumstances. It may be a silly and overused expression, but it is often claimed that *mahaddish biynam ga'an* (nobody in Egypt goes to bed hungry), implying that there is an unwritten system that allows things to function smoothly despite seeming haphazardness.

With corruption at its highest level in years, the only way to function is either on the lap of those in power or off the margins entirely, beyond the incompetence and reach of the state. In fact, it is this state's institutional inconvenience and incompetence that rendered it inconsequential and irrelevant. This shell that concealed the emptiness of the state was the fortified exoskeleton of the police and security forces, the intelligence agencies, the military, and other instruments of control and suppression. This shell is precisely what the revolution shattered, leaving little more than the empty container.

In fact, it is because of this phenomenon that the state both reacted disproportionately and then crumbled so swiftly, like a wafer, in the face of a massive uprising whose initial demand was a reformist one. The collapse of the state came at the heels of a unique configuration of forces, growing regime incompetence, a marked spike in labor action, civil disobedience, and community engagement across the country for much of the last six years.

It is for this reason that, almost without prior planning and through the arithmetic of chance and the fraternal spirit of the people, during the eighteen days, Tahrir Square and other similar locales across the country turned into microcosms of the country as clinics, schools, nurseries, bathrooms, eateries, and media centers replaced the state in the most extemporaneous way, as if this had been the case for a long time. When the police disappeared from the streets for seven straight months, the country did not descend into mayhem but rather remained largely safe and self-sustaining through the impromptu work of popular committees and other even less formal collectives.

Today, the government shows no signs of revival. Instead, Egyptians are settling into a state of minimalist functionality as political powers try to resuscitate the institutions. So, while there may be a cabinet in place, ministries working, and police deployed in the streets, revolutionary Egypt remains the largest experiment in self-government to date. Morsi is a powerless president. The elected parliament is incompetent, inactive, and without a mandate. The judiciary has not been independent of the executive and military branches for decades. And while SCAF wields tangible power, their management of the transition has destroyed whatever legitimacy and inter-institutional coherency they inherited from the old regime. So when SCAF accused various revolutionary groups of trying to dismantle the state, it came with some degree of irony, as this was essentially a self-fulfilling prophecy. The only way the system is able to assert itself despite its weakness is through political polarization, in many instances unnecessarily. For instance, in the presidential election runoff, fears on both sides reached a crescendo, both of which will prove to be unfounded, since Morsi and Shafiq, as far as the priorities of the revolution are concerned, will likely end up being two faces of the same coin. And despite the fearmongering ahead of the election, 49 percent of eligible Egyptians did not vote in the first open contested presidential election.

What, then, has replaced the loose remnants of the state's institutions? Communitarian collectives and social reliance have come into play at the local level and are moving up concentrically, both on a geographic scale and across economic, class, political, and religious divides. I would argue this is but one manifestation of Egypt's increasingly recognizable anarcho-syndicalism, a system of informal collective self-rule that supplants the state where it can no longer function. I am not making a case for the durability of such a model of governance in Egypt, but merely stating that this has been the trend (in varying degrees across the country) over the past decade. Consistent with the revolutionary discourse and preexisting governance formations in Egypt, the discourse of self-rule is one that institutions are simply incapable of comprehending, absorbing, communicating with, learning from, or emulating.

I have grown fond of the way French philosopher Alain Badiou addresses this phenomenon in his book *Metapolitics*, where he sees the origin of true politics as outside the framework of reconnecting bonds and chiasms or the search for a more representative and democratically accountable government. Instead, for Badiou as for Egypt, politics is about the meticulous unbinding of the democratic representative system. With SCAF pushing Egypt into eight rounds of elections in fifteen months, there is a forceful intent to confirm electoral politics as the only means of expression acceptable. Sucking the life out of the unshackled and youthfully spontaneous spirit of Tahrir and other public spaces is an immediate intent. Another is to condition and institutionalize the public into relying upon the state for what it can no longer do.

In the end, the history of designing anything for Egypt has been a failure—from colonial imposition to structural adjustment programs and from aggressive electoral dynamics to political training workshops. In the same manner that the French Revolution gave us a reformation in the relationship between the ruler and the ruled, and the Russian Revolution gave us a different view of capital, production, and distribution, the Egyptian revolution is giving us a novel example of self-government. Those who came out in the millions across the country during the eighteen days and beyond have a gut instinct. It is in that gut instinct that the country's unpredictability lies. It is there that we derive our sense of optimism and our belief that a wrong can be righted. And it is there that fictitious democratic experiments are trumped by the power of what is naturally occurring.

New Face

August 18, 2012

On Monday morning, August 13, Field Marshal Tantawi woke up and didn't recognize himself in the mirror. Once the last man standing from Mubarak's coterie, his day had finally come. On Monday morning, President Muhammad Morsi woke up and didn't recognize himself in the mirror. Once the obedient, desperate choice of a perpetually vilified Muslim Brotherhood presidency, his day had finally come. On Monday morning, Egyptians woke up and didn't recognize themselves in the mirror. Once bound and destined to live under military rule, their day had finally come. On Monday morning, no one recognized their own faces.

Sociologist Erving Goffman spent a career analyzing how we use our faces as dynamic forms of symbolic representation and as communicative instruments. To him the face was a mask upon which we anchor our external selves, the part of us we'd like to reveal and behind which we keep what we'd like to conceal. Goffman described people's ability to read facial cues as a sign of competence. But what he had not considered is the absolute and irreversible inability to read any and all faces.

I learned of this condition some months ago at a genetics conference, where a German scientist described the case of a patient whose cerebral dysfunction made her incapable of identifying characteristics of the human face. Known as prosopagnosia (derived from the Greek words *prosopon*, meaning 'face,' and *agnosia*, 'not knowing'), the ailment leads to face-blindness. Patients are incapable of recognizing loved ones, friends, neighbors, popular figures, or celebrities. When they see someone's face, it seems as if they are meeting them for the very first time. Their features are unrecognizable. And in the most severe cases, they cannot recognize their own faces in photos or the mirror. Egypt on August 13 seemed unrecognizable to itself.

Many notable Egyptians have undergone facelifts, such as Mustafa Bakry and former member of parliament Muhammad Abu Hamid; some have simply switched roles, such as Ahmed Ezz and Khairat al-Shater (the faces of their respective parties' problematic commercial policies); and some have self-effaced, such as the still-influential former NDP cadres. For many months, since the toppling of Mubarak, we all suffered from prosopagnosia (incidentally, a dominant hereditary trait), as we wondered who ruled the country and who was calling the shots. Knowing full well that it wasn't the scar-faced revolutionaries, was it the faceless deep state, the defaced *fulul*, the two-faced Brotherhood, or the stone-faced SCAF?

Do we really know who anyone is any more? Who are Alaa Al Aswany, Naguib Sawiris, and Amr Moussa? Can we recognize the amorphous prime minister Hisham Qandil whose vacuous history renders him faceless? Do we know a technocrat when we see one? Or does being a technocrat necessitate being faceless and interchangeable? What about the now-recognizable facial signifiers such as the mask from *V for Vendetta*, the much-debated and increasingly omnipresent *niqab*, and ElBaradei's round-framed glasses? What have these facial signifiers come to mean in Egypt today?

What about the military institution? Is it the same after Monday? What do we know about the new minister of defense, General Abd al-Fatah al-Sisi? Is he the same person who publicly exonerated the virginity tests performed on protesters? What about his deputy, General Muhammad al-Assar? Can we identify him in a crowd? Could the face that assured the Americans in July 2011 that little had changed in Egypt after the toppling of Mubarak belong to the same person who engineered the ousting of Tantawi and Anan? Is the Brotherhood still the Brotherhood? Are they still the Islamist, collective, and revolutionary organization? Is their position on Palestine still the same? Are they still committed to the nationalist project of their forefather Hasan al-Banna? What about President Morsi? Is he the same person who promised a civic state and vice presidents who are women and Copts? Is he the president or simply the face of a Muslim Brotherhood executive branch? What becomes of the Egyptian state now? Is this a facelift, a neck tuck, or rhinoplasty? Do we know a coup when we stare it in the face? We didn't on February 11, 2011. Was the removal of the top brass on the night of August 12 a presidential coup? Or was it an attempt to preempt a coup by SCAF against Morsi? Or is it neither?

Egypt has been through many phases in its ancient and modern histories, some of which have transformed it almost beyond recognition. However, Egyptians are now choosing to slap on the country the mask of their choice, hoping it will make it more recognizable. The Nasserists, Salafis, seculars, cosmopolitans, elite bourgeoisie, minorities, and Brotherhood all believe in their own illusions of majority because of their facemasks. Perhaps that is why, more than ever before, we are circulating images of Egypt as we remember it or would like it to be, so that the country is increasingly multi-faced. A video of Suad Hosni on all fours singing to a cat, a 1931 photo of Sa'd Zaghlul Boulevard in Alexandria, and even the more contemporary images from the January 25 Revolution, all help us mask the country lest we realize that what we have before us bears no resemblance to our mental images. Alternatively, Islamist groups are circulating images from the 1920s and 1930s showing Cairene and Alexandrian women frequenting markets in face veils to authenticate the "true" conservative nature of Egyptian society. We nostalgically create and confirm these now-fictionalized faces of Egypt to our collective detriment. Without these faces that we recognize, we cannot identify, classify, assess, evaluate, record, and recall human experience. In short, we cannot function.

Instead Egypt should take a lesson from the esteemed primate biologist and psychologist Jane Goodall. Confronting her own prosopagnosia, she decided to spend much of her life with apes and chimpanzees because she need not know their faces; instead, she knew each one by his or her behavior. Starting Monday morning, per Goodall's approach, all actors in the Egyptian public polity must be judged by their behaviors, not their phenotypes. By overcoming our reliance on face-value judgments, we can stand face-to-face with our face-blindness.

Media Forms

August 30, 2012

I am no wordsmith but I have a fascination with language. I am no grumpy grammarian but I admire clean prose. I am no adherent to structure but I appreciate good form. As a self-confessed news junkie, I spend many hours of the day sifting through content and coverage, perusing dozens of publications, and essentially devouring news in bulk. This mind-numbing overexposure to Egyptian news media has alerted me to a palpable crisis in the country's journalistic form.

While I am particularly jubilant about the Egyptian media's newfound revolutionary impulse and the astounding margin of freedom already reached — taken by force and not bestowed by any sitting government — I am finding myself increasingly lamenting the demise of form. Whether it's the reporting of non-news such as an activist catching a flight from the United Arab Emirates to Cairo, a former parliamentarian visiting a mosque, or a negligible tweet from a pseudo-intellectual, a substantial proportion of content offers little to no insight whatsoever. On the other hand, the dearth in analysis has become so immense that in many instances the insatiable desire to scoop has turned news into an assembly line of capsule-sized incomprehensible meaninglessness that desecrates the lofty principles of journalism. A profession meant to inform is now in desperate need of reform, a discombobulated cacophony of disorder.

In a revolutionary milieu it is necessary to advocate for an end to conditionality and conformity, a shattering of crippling taboos and institutionalized decorum. It is an occasion to obliterate hierarchical thinking and intellectual patronage. A socially conscious, responsible journalism can indeed exist without formative structures. But perhaps it is my concern about form itself that is problematic. Form is not the rigid structure or the intransigently stubborn rules of journalistic practice such as the news world's 'inverted pyramid' or the television 'sound bite'—both being partially responsible for the end of audience commitment to knowledge, a blatant infantilization of citizens, and the enshrinement of a lowest common denominator. Instead, form is what makes something recognizable. What made media recognizable over the past sixty years of military rule was its uniformity and its conformity, both subsets of form. After January 25, the expectation of journalistic reformation quickly turned to deformity. More often than not, the news media, both state and private, embedded in their own respective political economic trenches, have done more to misinform than to inform.

So instead of a transformative competition over quality where journalistic entities attempt to outperform one another (to the public's benefit), we have a polarization that has transformed the media landscape and rendered it mediocre, haphazard, and increasingly narcissistic. The self-absorption of 'media narcissists' is enormous; anyone can become a celebrity if they are able to fit into the frivolous categories of *baltagi*, *fulul*, revolutionary, artist, youth, Islamist, and the like. While I am all for shattering the arrogance of self-ascribed political and economic renown, especially among Egypt's elite, the purposeless reification, deification, and vilification of every and any Egyptian in the media today is alarming and itself counterrevolutionary.

Tawfiq Okasha may not have deserved the notoriety he garnered for his television station al-Fara'in, but he should not be a victim of archaic forms of information control. *Al-Dustur* newspaper may not have violated Egypt's new revolutionary impulse by confronting the executive branch, but neither the publication nor its editor should be viewed as martyrs of a looming era of Islamist takeover of the media. Of course, further battles over freedom of the press will be waged in the months and years to come as the entire structure of governance convulses from the seismic shifts facing Egypt today. With the Muslim Brotherhood digging its claws deeper and deeper into the body of Egyptian state media, especially by appointing the editors in chief of state newspapers, and the private media sharpening their fangs for battles against the Islamists, any legislative or legal confrontation between these two camps will have long-lasting repercussions for journalism's form and could lay waste to the necessary plurality and occasionally healthy media discord imperative for a viable democracy.

The refreshing news is that the days of journalistic complacency are over. The intoxicating uniformity of authoritarian media seems long gone and the use of manufactured news as chloroform to anesthetize the public will no longer work for this generation. For those who fear that the Brotherhood will resurrect the media control of yesteryear, the writing on the wall is as revolutionary as cuneiform. What lies in wait for the formless fourth estate is a furious fixation with the newfound freedoms that promise a fecund future.

Lemons and Raisins

October 17, 2012

Yassin and Ali, both of Generation Tahrir, were embroiled in a heated argument before the presidential elections. "Shafiq will be impossible to depose. He will have the legitimacy of a free and fair election, the old regime on his side, and all backed by the military," pressed Ali. Yassin shook his head vigorously in dismay and rejection. "What the fuck are you talking about!" he barked back. "If Morsi comes to power, the Brotherhood will infiltrate all state institutions and with the power of religious language, they will win elections indefinitely!" They bickered on until the day of reckoning came. Ali had convinced Yassin to vote for Morsi by assuring him that even if the Muslim Brotherhood wanted to reconstitute the old regime structure, it would be inconceivable and impossible given Egypt's newfound revolutionary fervor. Morsi won by a narrow margin—a margin afforded to him by scores of Yassins, now commonly known as *butu' al-lamuna* (the lemon people). They are those revolutionaries who are described as having 'squeezed a lemon over themselves' (as a coping mechanism) by voting against their better judgment.

One hundred days later, with the country's economic indicators still in rapid decline, with little palpable change from the pre-election transition, with electricity and water luxuries afforded mostly to the affluent, and with seemingly haphazard domestic and foreign policy tracks for the country, the lemon people have become the accused. With every decision from the Muslim Brotherhood–led government to shut down a television network, fire an editor in chief, criminalize strikes, physically assault opposition protesters, incite against liberal activists, pressure the judiciary into submission, and steamroller non-Islamists in the drafting of the constitution, the lemon people lament their decision, which handed the government over to Morsi's Muslim Brotherhood.

There is no doubt that Egypt is in a far worse place now than at any point in its contemporary history, post-1967 war excepted. The combined political polarization and disenchantment has reached a crescendo as every current of opinion feels the country is slipping. The non-Islamist parties and fronts, notoriously weak and disorganized, have shown signs of life in the presidential elections as notables like Sabbahi and ElBaradei remain influential on the political scene. Nevertheless, they lack the groundswell, the discipline, the commitment, and the motivation to pose a serious enough threat to the Muslim Brotherhood unless the latter commits enough blunders to warrant the success of a haphazard alternative. It is fair to say that this is the lowest point thus far for the 'civil' (the Egyptian nomenclature for 'liberal' and 'secular,' given the public stigma associated with these two terms) political forces. In the coming months and years, their ability to mobilize both in protests and in voting will be tested to the limits. With every meagerly attended and misnamed *milyuniya* (million-person march) and every electoral loss, the Muslim Brotherhood will settle more comfortably and permanently into every branch of the state apparatus, thereby transforming public life into a version of the Brotherhood, and rehabilitating Egyptians into compliance. In the absence of organized campaigning and canvassing in every governorate, municipality, and neighborhood, the civic political forces' chances of competing against the Brotherhood and other Islamist political groups are remote.

And while the struggle for Egypt's state should be a competition over policies that prioritize alleviating the misery of the subjugated, the lexicon of power-hungry politicos is that of symbolism and sloganeering. How often and where the president prays is an issue of national concern and attention. Preachers aligned with the Brotherhood appear on television exulting over Morsi, already proclaimed leader of the Umma al-Arabiya wa-l-Islamiya (Arab and Islamic Nation), and calling on him to come down on his detractors, critics, and adversaries with an iron fist. And as if basking in the glow of preemptive heroism, Morsi manufactures a populist, dare one say Nasserist, moment, by ceremoniously driving in an open carriage along the track of Cairo Stadium before ninety thousand cheering members of his ruling Freedom and Justice Party on the anniversary of the October 6, 1973 War. And as if it weren't ironic enough that the very stadium that hosted this propagandistic extravaganza was the same place where the revolutionary

Ultras football fans ritualistically shouted down the police state for years, the invited attendees of the celebration included none other than Abbud al-Zumur, one of the people charged in the assassination of President Sadat, the very architect of this war being commemorated!

Despite seeming to have free reign in the country since Morsi's ascent and the departure of the top military brass, the ruling party doesn't have it so easy. The Muslim Brotherhood, accustomed to charitable social development projects targeting the poor, are unable to scale up their unsustainable initiatives to cover Egypt's growing impoverished class. With a scriptural and ritualized system of initiation and indoctrination that keeps their members loyal, agreeable, disciplined, and motivated, the Brotherhood cannot manage a disparate and heterogeneous Egyptian populace using the same tools without employing a strong-handed legal instrument and a ruthless police state. In the absence of any vision and with the appointment of an inexperienced so-called technocratic government, the Brotherhood regime has desperately stumbled back toward the tried and tested, albeit flawed, policies of the Mubarak era. Whether it is accepting World Bank and International Monetary Fund money without safeguards, maintaining strong and collaborative relations with an oppressive Israeli state at the expense of the Palestinians (despite the Brotherhood's hostile domestic rhetoric), failing to improve wages or create a conducive environment for tourism, attacking labor action, asphyxiating anti-government expression, reducing subsidies on basic necessities, maintaining chummy ties with the Americans and Saudis, or continuing enmity with Iran, the Brotherhood are essentially a Mubarak regime with a *zibiba* ('raisin,' or prayer mark) on their foreheads.

Whether they are hidden behind Gamal Mubarak's accentless English or Morsi's beard and *zibiba*, the policies are indistinguishably counter-revolutionary. However, in the post-Mubarak era, the *zibiba* goes a long way. Today signs of piousness and religiosity are emblems of the new regime. This is an administration whose rhetoric is adorned with Qur'anic verses, anecdotes from the Hadith, and religious salutations accenting every expression. To emulate this style, or at least adapt to its pervasiveness, is to be in sync with the tones and vernacular of power today. But tone and vernacular alone don't feed the hungry, treat the sick, educate children, or pay the bills.

The Salafis, once the darlings of the SCAF-led transition period and surprise placers in the parliamentary elections, have also hit the wall as their parties and movements become increasingly disorganized, their rhetoric becomes self-contradictory, and their violations and contradictions are exposed publicly. The one identifying feature that distinguishes them from their competition is their religious interpretations and their obsession with the imposition of *sharia* law. Today there are at least ten competing parties and visions that share this outlook as a platform, in some instances supporting one another and in other cases scandalizing one another. With the Brotherhood in power, the Salafis are caught in a bind—use their weight and popularity to serve as an opposition, or join ranks with the ruling party and retain the role of runners-up. However, both scenarios are excruciatingly risky. A sinking Brotherhood ship is one the Salafis would be best advised to avoid. Since they have no comprehensive plan of their own, the Salafis are desperate to benefit from the Brotherhood's plan.

In the coming period, and following the October 12 altercations between the two political camps in Tahrir, the prospects for both an empowered but weary Islamist camp and a debased but confident liberal front are in the balance. For either group to effectively prevail, they must first shake off the façade of their symbols. The lemon people, no longer benefiting from their strategic votes, cannot afford to continue camouflaging their political identity in the name of the 'common good.' And for those who proudly flaunt the raisin, it is their responsibility to represent far more than a trend, a party, or a dogma. With both groups having voted for the same president, and to whom this president owes justification for his faltering, it is their honest and transparent political will that Egypt so direly needs between now and the next round at the ballot.

Blood Ballots

December 31, 2012

Ten days before the March 2011 constitutional referendum, hundreds of soldiers went on a rampage in Tahrir Square, tearing up protesters' tents, arresting dozens, and torturing them on the premises of the Egyptian Museum. The protesters were opposing the military's monopoly of power, the continued presence of old regime figures, and the hasty patch-up of the constitution. Blood was spilled and no one was prosecuted.

Four days before the parliamentary elections, forty-seven protesters were killed, dozens lost an eye, and thousands were injured at the hands of the security forces on Muhammad Mahmud Street. Protesters were rallying against the police attack on martyrs' families and other demonstrators in Tahrir Square and the rush to parliamentary elections under military rule. Blood was spilled and no one was prosecuted.

Six days before the constitution was put to the vote, eight people were declared dead and dozens severely injured following a violent attack by supporters of the president on protesters camping in front of the Ittihadiya Palace. Protesters were at the presidential palace to challenge President Muhammad Morsi's constitutional declaration that rendered him omnipotent and his speedy push to put the Islamist constitution to a referendum. Blood was spilled and no one was prosecuted.

With the country polarized as at no time in its recent history, the parliamentary elections commencing in two months will likely be preceded by more waves of violence between two camps, both claiming to speak for the revolution.

Since the toppling of Hosni Mubarak, an intractable relationship between blood and ballots has been forged. Elections are held in the name of this blood. Politicians advocate on behalf of this blood. Brotherhoods and parties procure voters on the grounds of honoring this blood. Clerics speak of sacrificing more of this blood. And government officials claim reforms are necessary to avoid adding to this blood.

As the second anniversary of the revolution nears, those who sacrificed to make it happen are no closer to ruling than they were when it started. Nevertheless, everyone speaks for the revolution, shouts its now commodified slogans, and contorts its principles. The political status quo—both the Muslim Brotherhood and the state apparatus—are sending a clear message to Egyptians: Blood spilled in the streets can only be redeemed in the ballot box. The blood that made their ascendancy possible has now been reduced to symbolic ink stains on the voters' fingers.

"That which is gained by the ballot box can only be lost in the ballot box." But what of that which was lost in the streets, in the minds, in the hearts, in the souls? With every passing day, we discover the growing gulf between the revolution's aspirations and the plans of those who claim to speak for it. The masses, increasingly disenchanted by an empty political process, are participating in declining numbers in one vote after the other. Voters and non-voters alike realize the country's future is a battle between two minorities—one idealistic and revolutionary and the other political and opportunist. One donates blood and the other reaps it.

With the Egyptian calendar now filled with bloodied commemorations, it would be wise for all to heed the lesson of the past two years: Ballots do not blot blood.

A Nation Derailed

January 28, 2013

Just ten days before the second anniversary of the January 25 Revolution, Egyptians awoke to another railway tragedy. A train loaded beyond its capacity with security forces recruits heading from Sohag to Cairo derailed in the Badrashin area of Giza, leaving nineteen dead and over 120 injured, adding to the toll of deaths on train tracks in Egypt. It was only a month earlier that a rushing train in Asyut obliterated a bus full of children, killing fifty of them.

In the late night hours of January 14, Badrashin was awoken by the news of the tragedy. Those who had arisen to attend to their morning prayers were called upon to act as rescue workers to save the many who were trapped under the train. In a span of minutes, residents of the nearby areas began to stream out of their homes to help at the site of the incident. Under the cover of darkness, with makeshift lighting, the people of Badrashin performed heroics in the absence of any state intervention. They were picking up the bodies of the deceased, collecting their belongings, attending to the injured, and collectively attempting to lift tons of twisted metal with their bare hands to save those trapped underneath the body of the train. The absence of the state's emergency and transportation service was ominously eerie.

In Egypt, like anywhere else, accidents happen. But in Egypt, they happen again, and again, and again, and yet again. The Badrashin incident will likely not be the last of the train tragedies in a country where the national average has become one railroad catastrophe per month. What is even more worrisome than the knowledge of impending disaster is the inanities of those who either do not know of it or actively conceal it. A newly minted minister of transportation took a call from a television station on the morning of the Badrashin bloodshed. He mumbled through the answers, said nothing about rescue teams being available on site, and lazily ignored the calls for heavy vehicles to lift the body of the train to rescue survivors, relayed to him by the anchor. Lacking in any sympathy, or even token commiseration, the minister's tone spoke to the obliviousness of those in power today in Egypt.

The nearby Hawamdiya Hospital was the recipient of the injured soldiers. Understaffed, underserviced, unsanitary, and woefully ill equipped to handle such an influx of emergency cases, the hospital staff left the young soldiers strewn throughout the rooms, sometimes two to a bed. The images circulating online and in the news of their pain and misery at the hospital shone some light on a facility that would have otherwise never been given any distinct attention. Not only was the country's ailing railway system on display, its healthcare institutions, laid to waste by the double punch of decades of systematic neglect and worsening mismanagement under the Morsi government, were in full view.

So cataclysmically destructive was this incident for the government's public image that they moved swiftly to try and counter the barrage of negative media coverage. President Morsi was rushed to Maadi Military Hospital in Cairo, where some of the injured had allegedly been transferred. He posed for photos with the injured in the comparatively advanced, clean, and presentable medical facility so as to showcase the exceptional treatment being offered to the recruits. The president's office subsequently distributed these photos to the press corps for wide dissemination. Prime Minister Hisham Qandil, also on site, had his photo taken while donating blood. This too was distributed by the prime minister's office to the media. The benevolent charity of the state and its leadership were in full gear to counter what was otherwise a public-relations disaster for the government. Yet the damage had already been done. The public had heard the cries live from Badrashin on the private television network ONTV (which some Muslim Brotherhood members suggested had a hand in the accident, due to their prompt presence on site before other networks) and seen the photos from Hawamdiya Hospital.

On the second anniversary of the Day of Rage, January 28, 2011, when Egypt's uprising reached a crescendo that permanently changed the political map of the country, it feels as if derailment is less of a symptom of the railway sector, and more of a condition afflicting the state. As its institutions stubbornly cling to corruption and approximation, its new leaders are setting new standards of negligence, incompetence, and disingenuous political posturing. It seems today's authorities are more concerned with varnishing their image than developing a systematic plan to change. Attempting, in any way, to deflect attention away from its disastrous mismanagement of both the country and national tragedies, the government's 'mother ship,' the Muslim Brotherhood, has often resorted to distraction through divisive identity politics and sectarianism. Various Muslim Brotherhood members and affiliated groups have openly suggested that these frequent railway tragedies are intentional acts by Christians. More recently, the Brotherhood has also described the Black Bloc, a newcomer to the Egyptian protest scene fashioned after similar anonymous dissident groups worldwide, as a Christian militia.

However, the Black Bloc are not divorced from Egypt's railways, not because of the false claim that they share a confessional faith with the train drivers, but rather because their first actions alongside the Ultras and other groups were largely focused on blocking train traffic in the country. On several occasions—two days before the January 25 anniversary, and the three consecutive days leading up to the Day of Rage memorials—the Black Bloc placed their bodies on the train tracks and brought the railroads to a standstill. Similar revolutionary groups closed down several metro lines and blocked traffic on the 6 October Bridge and other arteries in the country.

As battles rage on in Port Said, Suez, Cairo, Alexandria, and elsewhere for more reasons than can be reviewed here, there is a general sentiment that the country's revolution is not only outside the offices of power, it has been irreparably derailed. The myriad forms of civil disobedience occurring across the country today, which President Morsi vowed to counter decisively, speak to more than a commemoration of a bygone era of tyranny. In no mood to celebrate, Egyptians are revolting against political monopolization, the continuation of a defunct economic policy, an empty state discourse of embellishment, the radical deprofessionalization of the public-service sector, and, of course, the country's "trains of death." Two years have passed since anger swept the country and shook the world. With Morsi in the driver's seat, the so-called "renaissance train," as the Muslim Brotherhood often calls its multifaceted modernization project, is now no more than a sick joke. Little remains of this misnomer besides twisted irony and, in response, depressing satire. In Egypt's streets today, curfews are being violated, reinstated emergency laws are being ignored, and the state's overt threats seem to intimidate no one. While the government accuses protesters of derailing the country's progress and development, it is evident to most that it was Morsi who had driven this train off the tracks.

Epilogue

I met GemyHood in Casablanca, Morocco in October 2012. A jack-of-all-trades, Gemy (whose real name is Mohammed Beshir) had tried his hand at everything and seen plenty in thirty-two short years. He was a singer, dancer, actor, filmmaker, editor, author, activist, musician, teacher, poet, traveler, and obsessive football fan. Now known mostly for his solidarity with and writings on the Ultras—fanatical football fans whose passion for the game and opposition to its corporatization are no less strong than their antagonism toward the police state—Gemy has found himself embroiled in many of their battles.

The Ultras fans of both of the Cairo giants al-Ahly and Zamalek, and other teams as well, assumed the role of revolutionary foot soldiers throughout the eighteen days of protest that toppled Mubarak and beyond. They have lost many in their ranks and dealt the greatest blows to the security apparatus of the state. Battle-scarred and experienced, they have become a complicated symbol of heroism and mourning on one side, and an emblem of radical fraternity and unpredictable combustibility on the other. Impeccably organized, dogmatically loyal, committedly local, decidedly leaderless, and fiercely anonymous, the Ultras are perhaps the first openly spontaneous, egalitarian, organized, collective, anarchic, and revolutionary movement in contemporary Egypt.

Gemy came to Casablanca to lead training workshops for young Arabs from across the region on human rights and activism to fight corruption in their respective countries. But behind the façade of Gemy, the artistic polymath and charismatic educator is a deeply shaken soul. He barely sleeps at night and wakes up with nightmares that leave him debilitated. Every morning before his sessions, Gemy suffered short-term paralysis that left him unable to speak or move his arms for several hours. When asked about his symptoms, he recounted the days on the front lines of the Muhammad Mahmud Street battles, and blames them for his psychological trauma. With his eyes tearing up, Gemy retold the story of being rained on with tear gas and birdshot as he and a friend were on the ground. By the time he looked up, his friend had been shot in the head and he himself had narrowly escaped with a few pellets lodged in his hat. On the same day, his friend and blogger Malek X had lost an eye, and dentist and activist Ahmad Harara lost his second eye (the first he lost on the Day of Rage, January 28, 2011, at the hands of Mubarak's police). Imagining that moment, Gemy started crying and could not be consoled.

His anguish might have been tempered had he not felt that Egypt as he knew it was being pulled from underneath him and his friends, brethren, and comrades. Throughout the day, Gemy would often utter the words "*al-balad rahit, ya gidan!*" ("The country is gone, folks!"). It is this country, that he watched his friends die to liberate and lose their eyes to awaken, that was being stolen from them. The country they had fought to empower was disempowering them. Gemy agonized over the extent to which Egypt had become tolerant of its intolerance and ignorant of its ignorance.

It would be an understatement to say that the current regime of the Muslim Brotherhood has broken the spirit of many revolutionaries, like Gemy and the Ultras. The Brotherhood did so not by defeating them, but by irresponsibly adopting their lingo, absorbing their vernacular, engulfing their demands, and wearing them as a cloak to legitimize themselves, while wholly abandoning their ideals. They carried the banner of the revolution after excising the revolutionaries from it. And aside from disenchanting the young and often impressionable revolutionary youth, the Brotherhood cabinet has done little to lift the country out of its abysmal human-rights state and in some instances even aggravated it.

It was Morsi's minister of education who gave an interview to a television network defending the beating of students in schools. It was also under the Brotherhood's tenure that a school principal who believed and advocated that his teachers enforce Islamic customs by coercing girls to wear the hijab went unpunished. And it was a top woman official and legislator in the Freedom and Justice Party who argued that the enforcement of a legal age for marriage was problematic as it interfered with what she described as the "desire of young women" (as early as nine years old) to wed upon reaching puberty. She made her case using an amalgam of interpretations of the Qur'an and the Hadith and what she said were reports from the field. She argued that it would be a safeguard against deviant sexual behavior, premarital sex, pregnancy out of wedlock, and single motherhood. And it is with the Brotherhood in the driver's seat that the Ministry of Health turned a blind eye to the mushrooming of medico-religious quackery such as centers for treatment with camel urine. It was under Morsi's watch that liberal political figures such as Mohamed ElBaradei and Hamdeen Sabbahi were accused by Brotherhood operatives as traitors, infidels, or apostates, and in one case an ultraconservative cleric contorted a Hadith to call for the opposition leaders' heads. At no previous time has there been such a palpable stigma associated with such words as 'liberal' and 'secular,' now considered profanities and a death sentence for any political career.

Rhetoric aside, the Muslim Brotherhood government has also gone to great lengths to reinforce the same aggressive entrepreneurial policy and venture-capitalist values that set the Mubarak regime on a downward spiral. The Brotherhood's accusations against protests and labor strikes indicate a propensity to repeat old mistakes, a lack of vision, and failure to attend to public needs. They have done very little to reduce capital flight from the country, as the general climate is discouraging of investment, both foreign and domestic. And the flight from Egypt is human as well as capital. There is a slow and damaging exodus of minds, expertise, and hope. The tourism industry has been laid to waste in a very short two years and the novel "revolutionary tourism" cannot flourish unless the revolution itself prevails.

By winning the presidential elections and ramming through a constitution, the Brotherhood are now armed with the intransigent irrefutability of religious dogma, a legal arsenal in a constitution they engineered, a near-complete monopoly of the political order (from executive to legislative), and decades of popular psychic and educational estrangement that was manufactured by the Mubarak era. This was in fact his most generous gift to the Islamists. He handed them a faltering society whose public education system was catastrophically poor, whose exposure to media was deeply damaging, and whose intellectual curiosity had been effectively obliterated.

When it comes to geostrategic parameters and foreign policy in the post-Mubarak period, the Brotherhood have scored the trifecta necessary to ensure their survival in the region — U.S. endorsement and the promise of non-obstruction, Saudi and Qatari financial support, and Israeli cooperation. In return, the Americans expect Morsi to rein in anti-American hostility from more radical groups such as al-Qaeda and to moderate the Salafi groups in the country, to push Hamas toward recognizing and cooperating with Israel, to use the Brotherhood's outreach to secure a stable, post-Assad, non-*jihadi* Syria, and to maintain distance from Iran. The Saudis persuaded the Brotherhood to tone down their activity in the Gulf and Jordan, fragile monarchies that can easily succumb to a populist Islamist movement. The Qataris are happy to have backed the winning horse for once, and continue to do so through investments and loans to prop up the Brotherhood and the country's economy during Morsi's tenure, as well as through Al Jazeera Mubasher Misr—an Arabic, Egypt-focused, overwhelmingly pro-Brotherhood channel launched post-Mubarak. The Israelis are comfortable with a stable and predictable southwestern border, where the ruling Islamists themselves are the ones policing the territory and their hostility to the Zionist state is limited to the usual regimen of ritualized rambling rhetoric and fiery fervor unmatched by action.

With the Americans throwing their money and support behind every institution and political group in the country—from the military to the anti-military NGOs—it is difficult for any one of them to convincingly accuse another of being America's agent or collaborator. The Egyptian military remains one of the biggest recipients of aid from the United States, and its top generals received their education and instruction from American academies. Similarly, many human-rights and civil-society organizations in Egypt rely heavily on U.S. funding to survive—although the Bush administration was far more generous than the Obama administration, which decided to dry up these funds. And perhaps more surprisingly for some, even the top ranks of the Brotherhood have been courted by, and have themselves courted, the United States.

President Morsi grew out of a U.S.-based lineage, having spent many of his formative years in the Brotherhood's American network. While it is publicly uncouth to state this explicitly, it should come as no surprise to any observer of regional politics in the last decade that prominent Brothers have established close relations with the U.S. State Department. Most notable of these is the Los Angeles–based Hatout family, who have made significant inroads toward creating a haven for the Muslim Brotherhood in the United States and became close confidants of the White House during the Bill Clinton and George W. Bush presidencies. With everyone implicated, accusations of association with the United States are a fire that will burn every party in the Egyptian polity, making America a major player in the country's domestic and regional politics in the future.

This contradiction leads to an irony in the way the Egyptian government under Morsi manages such affairs—both admonishing and praising the same parties, or critiquing foreign policies while upholding the same policies. For example, Egyptian security forces sought to take credit, and American gratitude, for tracking down and killing an armed man thought to be involved in the September 11, 2012 attack on the U.S. diplomatic mission in Benghazi, Libya, which claimed the life of Ambassador Christopher Stephens. Ironically, it was the Muslim Brotherhood who encouraged, both online and offline, the participation of Egyptians in protests against the controversial film *Innocence of Muslims* and directed the anger of the public toward the U.S. embassy.

Another example is that of Morsi's letter of credence to Israeli president Shimon Peres accompanying the appointment of a new ambassador. The letter—which, in Morsi's defense, is indeed protocol—was leaked by the Israeli presidency to showcase the overly mushy language used by the Brotherhood head of state in addressing the top official of Egypt's long-time adversary Israel. Morsi and the Muslim Brotherhood struggled to explain why its political leader described the head of Zionist Israel as a "great and good friend" and closed the letter with the words "highest esteem and consideration." Just a few years ago, the heads of the Brotherhood called for the eviction of the Israeli ambassador to Egypt, and they supported the protests outside the Israeli embassy in the summer of 2011. And while Morsi insists to Egyptians that the Camp David accords with Israel are unjust and must be amended, if not abolished, he continues to assure U.S. officials and prominent visitors, such as former president Jimmy Carter, that the treaty "will not change unless Israel wants [it] to." These are just a few example of the Egyptian government's Janus-faced approach to politics and the public under the Muslim Brotherhood. It is probably the reason why some of the fastest-growing Facebook groups in Egypt today are those that incriminate the Muslim Brotherhood. In the same tradition as the novel *'Askar Kazibun* (Military Liars) campaign against SCAF's propaganda, a similar mobilization is underway against Morsi, his party, and the Brotherhood, known as *Ikhwan Kazibun* (Brotherhood Liars).

Yet the Muslim Brotherhood itself is not the greatest worry for Egypt's nascent revolutionary movement and its hopeful utopian adherents. Instead it is the marriage of aggressive disaster capitalism with a theocratic doctrine and a strong-handed statism that would be a catastrophe for both the revolution and the country at large. It is this cocktail that makes the new Egyptian polity appear as a rigid entity that does not respect its own Muslim denominations (such as the Sufis and Shi'a), let alone its Christians, its foreign visitors, its tourists, and its expatriates.

Another problem is the abundance of hegemonic institutions in Egypt, including the intelligence agencies, which have operated in absolute secrecy in Egyptian society to contain dissent and undermine the political adversaries of the ruling NDP. With the revolution, there appears to be a tussle between the branches of security within the state and their loyalty to various sectors of power, from SCAF to the judiciary to the police apparatus to military intelligence to economic behemoths, seen and unseen. Now that anyone in the limelight is going to be demolished, it is no secret that the state's most influential asset holders are digging themselves deeper trenches so as to disappear from the public eye. The death of Omar Suleiman, Egypt's security and intelligence chief, will not end the deep state's obscurity, but rather hide it further from reach, as the keys to Egypt's back-door policies are buried with him. Hegemony in Egypt has a new face, new leadership, and a new language. It speaks of revolution while suppressing it, it speaks of reform while reversing it, it speaks of freedom while restraining it, and it speaks of renaissance while aborting it. Arguably, Mubarak's Egypt was in the process of transmogrifying from a tyrannical state to a hegemonic one until it was rudely interrupted by the revolution. Today that process is back on track as the revolution serves as a rhetorical tool to rationalize the perfection of hegemony. And with the Brotherhood in charge, these institutions can sink deeper into secrecy.

All the while, the awakened elite remain woefully out of touch with the communities they hope to reach. While leftist parties are slowly connecting with the concerns of society's downtrodden, especially in the factories and the working class, they are still light-years behind the Muslim Brotherhood and the Salafis. Many self-proclaimed liberal revolutionary groups remain either adamant or camouflaged neoliberals who are unable to overcome their bourgeois values and sensibilities. Some split their time between Tahrir, their suburban mansions, and their beachside villas. If their well-intentioned political actions are a drop in a bucket, their economic policies are a hole in that bucket. And while their values and priorities are supported by a large subset of the population, their resistance to institutionalization does not bode well.

And even if nothing described thus far about Egypt's trajectory were worrisome, the manner in which the country's constitution was devised deserves mourning. Once thought to be the only safeguard against tyranny, the document meant to chart the country's future and determine the relationship between the branches of government and citizens has effectively been hijacked by one constituency, the Brotherhood and other Islamist groups, at the expense of the rest of the country's population. By actively pursuing the application of *sharia* as law, not as principle, the constitution ventures where few other Muslim countries' founding documents go. Indonesia's constitution from 1945 has no mention of *sharia* as a result of a popular referendum that chose to discard this clause. The closest to Egypt's draft constitution is Pakistan's 1973 constitution, which declares Islam the state religion but defines Muslims as those who believe in the "absolute and unqualified finality" of the Prophet Muhammad. This laid the groundwork for systematic discrimination against two million Ahmadis, who believe that the nineteenth-century teacher Mirza Ghulam Ahmad was the last prophet of Islam.

Arguably, the most recent iteration of the constitution, a highly problematic document in almost every respect, greatly resembles the 1990 Cairo Declaration on Human Rights in Islam, which tried to merge and triangulate between Islamic law and the United Nations Declaration of Human Rights. This document attempted to introduce *sharia* into every clause in the declaration, but was considered to "gravely threaten the intercultural consensus on which international human rights instruments are based" (International Commission for Jurists' response to the Cairo Declaration presented to the UN Commission on Human Rights in 1992). Today's draft constitution eerily resembles the Cairo Declaration, which should cause everyone alarm.

And while constitutions often take months and years to draft, deliberate over, amend, and then bring to a public referendum, the Egyptian constitution was rushed through the pipeline. This rushing has only ruined it further. A document that was supposed to remedy glaring problems of injustice in Egypt is instead a foul-tasting medication. Rather than helping to legislate our freedoms, it curbs most of them. No better expression exists to describe this draft than *gih yikahlha 'amaha* (he tried to beautify her with make-up and ended up blinding her). As legal experts, clerics, jurists, and the media spend endless hours over the coming weeks, months, and years attempting to make sense of the document's applicability to daily life in Egypt, the product is likely to strain the legal system beyond its limits. The constitution's overzealousness and often-forced incorporation of the *sharia* will keep the country's legal institutions occupied for years to come. In the end, it will likely have one of two outcomes. It may become the seed for future theocratic authoritarianism—if not political, then sociocultural. Alternatively, it may become so impractical, dogmatic, and unworkable that it produces legal cobwebs that render the entire country extra-constitutional.

Since January 25, most structures have been subject to scrutiny and comparison. If anything, the revolution was a victory for revisionist history. From the military's fall from grace, to the illumination of the Muslim Brotherhood, to the questioning of once-accepted truths about war, peace, and presidencies, all institutions are now operating under the watchful and judgmental eye of public engagement. Every era is being contemplated and reconsidered with a new barometer. The public today demands meritocracy, and challenges the old 1960s ideal of *ahl al-thiqa* (the loyal) over *ahl al-kafa'a* (the competent). The culture of subservience, which was once slowly dissipating, has now been reversed. Today the Muslim Brotherhood still chooses the loyal over the competent, thereby reproducing the old regime.

It is this loyalty that precipitated the Ittihadiya attacks that led to the documented torture of anti-Morsi protesters on the palace grounds at the hands of members of the Muslim Brotherhood with the cooperation of police authorities. This incident revealed the degree to which Brotherhood members and their allies are prepared to go to confront their unarmed adversaries and use extreme violence against them for the sake of political power. It was also the first time the fracture in the relationship between young revolutionaries' groups that had fought the Mubarak regime together in Tahrir was large enough to pit them against one another in deadly encounters over the presidency. Islamist and non-Islamist revolutionaries, once indistinguishable brothers, were killing one another in front of the palace. Even the tight-knit Ultras were not immune to fracture as they fought one another at the palace door. Loyalty trumped friendship, allegiance overcame camaraderie, and affiliation muted memories.

Sadly, it is unipolarity that the Muslim Brotherhood is pushing for during their time in power. One example is the attempt by the government to reign in the populace in Cairo (the city that never sleeps). A shocking draft law proposed by General Ahmed Zaki Abdin, the minister of domestic development, would make it illegal to sell anything past midnight. When he was interviewed to explain the new law, one which is certifiably incompatible with Egyptian realities, he argued the doctrine was necessary because "we must teach the people discipline." Similarly, on the second anniversary of the revolution, with anti-Brotherhood demonstrations erupting across the country (especially in Port Said after the verdict on the football massacre in the city the previous year was handed down), dozens of people were killed by the police as the latter attempted to quell protests. In a moment of decisiveness and in the hope of assertively deterring further action in the restive city, Morsi threateningly reinstated the Emergency Law and imposed a curfew on the canal cities of Port Said, Suez, and Ismailia. The public's response came swiftly, valiantly, and dismissingly. Tens of thousands descended into the squares, broke the curfew, taunted Morsi, held public weddings, played pick-up football into the late hours of the night, and performed acts of civil disobedience for weeks. They had rendered the president's decision meaningless and unenforceable. In doing so, they had dealt his executive authority a major blow.

What the authorities in Egypt do not understand is what Badiou describes as "the political breakdown of community [bringing] about the right conditions for collective intellectual work." It is this breakdown that is the only determinant of what is objectively positive for the community. So if Abdin's law or Morsi's curfew are incompatible with the community, then they are negligible decrees, reserved solely for the books.

In the end, and against all odds, strikes and civil protest actions abound in Egypt and continue unabated. Legal processes are slowly being enacted to criminalize any protest that disrupts the function of the state. The most recent are the doctors' strikes, which take place because the hospitals are not secure and are often attacked by armed thugs. The doctors' wages are less than those of farmers and they are overworked due to the extremely heavy traffic of patients. The resources and supplies in the public healthcare sector are verging on squalor. Syringes have to be reused, garbage piles up outside the clinics, and the plumbing often breaks down, leaving sewer water running through the hospitals. The doctors protested for days without any response whatsoever from the government. So they have begun to resign. Similar actions were taken by students and faculty at Nile University and the American University in Cairo, along with other sectors and industries, from textile to natural gas, from steel to waterworks. In the end, virtually no industry has been unaffected by public action. And the government has done little to find a reasonable recourse for any of these challenges. So what started in the industrial town of Mahalla in 2008 continues like clockwork, as if the revolution and three rounds of elections had never occurred. Two of the three demands of the revolution—bread, freedom, and social justice—are not priorities for the sitting government. The policies of the Muslim Brotherhood continue to privilege free-market enterprise over subsidies for the poor. Improving foreign investment remains an obsession for the government in the midst of rising unemployment and inflation. And despite the remarkable expansion of the margin of freedom for expression and the press enjoyed in Egypt today, attempts to curb or silence critical media continue unabated.

So as the Islamists continue to perfect performance at the ballot box, and with curbs on freedom being enacted from the constitution down to individual laws, there has always been the hope that the practices of Mubarak's police state could not possibly be repeated under Islamists who themselves have been victims of decades of the most dehumanizing treatment for their political views and ambitions. In less than a year of Brotherhood rule, these expectations seem to have evaporated, as reports of torture and killing of opposition activists at police stations and facilities proliferate from across the country. The rights of women to participate in public space are dwindling, as organized sexual violence is used as a weapon of political intimidation. Anarchism and revolutionary fervor, especially in their recent iterations like the Black Bloc, become scapegoats to contain and streamline protests while using state violence against detractors ahead of economic downfall. Responsibility is distributed among an unreformed, sadistic police force, a power-hungry Muslim Brotherhood, a politically unreadable military establishment, and an opaque deep state.

In writing the essays in this book, I am acutely aware of their limitations. First and foremost, this volume is rife with romanticism. This is a tone I could not avoid, given the topsy-turvy nature of revolution and the remarkably stubborn optimism that continues to drive the embattled movement despite the consecutive blows. The essays in this volume were not meant to chart a moment or forecast anything to come. I know very well that my observations may not stand the test of time and I am happy to stand corrected on many of my reflections. These are not remedies or revelations, just musings and meditations. They are also limited to Egypt even though the country doesn't exist in a vacuum.

The general tone of the book is multipolar and quite disjointed—and it was designed to be so. It is neither Islamist, Coptic, secular, Marxist, socialist, ageist, liberal, communist, nor Salafi. While it is contemporary, it is mindful of history. And while trying to historicize, the frequent references to various moments in Egypt's past are not meant to suggest continuity or to telescopically flatten temporality, implying revolutionary lineage. This period is unique and familiar, exceptional but relatable.

My writings here are at once both universalist and relativist. It is humanism that may have forced me to perpetually overlook division and discord and instead focus on the overarching patterns and problems, in many instances to the detriment of my argument. In the end, this book is meant to historicize but not serve as a work of history, describe but not document, and narrate but not curate the Egyptian revolution. Admittedly, it is disorganized, amateur, and improvised, much like the revolution with which it is in dialogue. If anything, it is this very disorganization that is an homage to the endless struggle against unipolarity—the last refuge of desperate despots.

The lessons of Egypt's unfinished revolution are plenty. Do not celebrate preemptively. Do not valorize and glamorize the personhood of political leadership. Do not trust state authority to reform state institutions. Do not allow ideological rhetoric to guide your views irrespective of observable contradictions. Do not count on elections for deliverance. Do not expect allies of your once authoritarian adversary to serve your best interests. Always question pragmatic realist politics. Acknowledge and constantly challenge preexisting counterrevolutionary tendencies in the rhetoric of revolution. Do not lose sight of the subaltern, irrespective of the shifting contours of power. Always question identity-based populism even if it seems convenient or makes sense in a moment of false epiphany. Even when they sound transcendental, humans do not speak for deities. And lastly, look up and discover Omar Salah, the thirteen-year-old boy who sold sweet potatoes in Tahrir and had done nothing to deserve the deadly bullets of a soldier on the second anniversary of Mubarak's toppling. It is the Omars of Egypt that this revolution must answer to. It is the Omars of Egypt who will decide whether and when this revolution is finished.

Key People and Events

Abbasiya Clashes that occurred in the heavily fortified Abbasiya area of Cairo on July 23, 2011, where protesters were met by a military barricade and assailants from the neighborhood. This incident led to the death of one person and the injury of dozens.

Abd al-Fatah al-Sisi Minister of defense appointed by Muhammad Morsi in August 2012.

Abd al-Mun'im Abu al-Futuh Prominent former Muslim Brotherhood politician who ran as an independent in the first round of the presidential elections and came in fourth. He is the founder and head of the Strong Egypt Party.

Abougreisha Prominent Egyptian footballing family from the city of Ismailiya.

al-Ahly (football club) Egypt's and Africa's most popular and successful football club, based in Cairo.

Ahmad al-Fishawi Young Egyptian actor who was at the center of a scandal surrounding paternity for a child out of wedlock.

Ahmad al-Sawi Young independent songwriter credited with the profane revolutionary song "A7a ya thawra."

Ahmad Shafiq Mubarak's last prime minister and former minister of civil aviation. He resigned shortly after SCAF took over from Mubarak in February 2011. He was runner-up in the presidential elections, where he secured 47 percent of the vote.

Ahmed Ezz Egypt's top steel magnate, billionaire, and former official in the now dissolved NDP. He is in custody serving several sentences and faces further charges of corruption during his time in the leadership of the NDP.

Alaa Al Aswany Dentist-turned-novelist, he is a political activist and columnist often associated with the liberal political camp and the National Salvation Front.

Amr al-Bunni Young security employee at Cairo's opulent Nile Stars Towers, who became involved in an altercation at work over unpaid wages in early August 2012. He was shot and killed by the Towers' guards, leading to clashes between security, police, and protesters outside the buildings.

Amr Moussa Veteran Egyptian diplomat who held the position of minister of foreign affairs under Mubarak. He also served as the secretary general of the Arab League. Moussa was a presidential candidate in 2012 and was eliminated in the first round of voting after placing fifth overall.

April 6 Youth Movement A rights- and justice-oriented youth activist group that began in solidarity with labor actions in the industrial city of Mahalla in 2008. Gaining prominence online and offline, the group was instrumental in mobilizing on the ground ahead of January 25. Despite splintering into several groups, they remain an integral part of the revolutionary front.

Ayman Nour Prominent opposition politician and lawyer who started the al-Ghad party. He ran in the first contested election against Mubarak in 2005 and was runner-up. He was then imprisoned and later pardoned by Mubarak. He remains a prominent yet polarizing political figure in the post-Mubarak era.

Balloon Theater incident An attack by police on the families of martyrs at the site of the Balloon Theater in Cairo on June 29, 2011 led to clashes between protesters and security forces, causing the injury of 590 people.

Battle of the Camel The iconic afternoon of February 2, 2011 when Mubarak supporters and paid camel- and horse-keepers from the Nazlit al-Simman area near the pyramids descended on Tahrir Square to attack protesters there and break up their sit-in. The incident was widely televised and thought to be one of the more scandalous and internationally damaging for the Mubarak regime throughout the eighteen days of protests. The question of who incited, funded, and supported the attack remains hotly contested in Egypt.

Cabinet sit-in incident On December 16, 2011 a protracted sit-in in front of the Cabinet building calling for the end of military reign, the removal of the government, and the transfer of power to a presidential council was met with brutal force by the police authorities, leading to a rapid escalation of violence that left dozens dead and hundreds injured.

The military police were sent in to empty Tahrir square violently. Photographs and videos shot during this attack had wide repercussions internationally, especially footage of an anonymous young woman (now known as "Tahrir Girl" and "Blue Bra Girl") being stripped and beaten.

Chilean miners Between August 5 and October 13, 2010, international media were dominated by the story of Chilean miners trapped underground. Global news attention was captivated by the arduous efforts to rescue them.

'deep state' A nebulous term used to describe the amalgam of political and economic interests within both the state institutional structure and the financial power centers, and their ability to insulate themselves from public purview. Most often used to characterize the level of invisibility of agencies and apparatuses that act in concert and impose themselves on government and popular discourses without being accountable. In Egypt, the deep state is believed to comprise intelligence agencies, opaque economic powerhouses, top-tier actors on behalf of the military establishment, and select influence-wielding ruling party operatives. The Turkish example of the deep state is the most frequently mentioned in the Middle East.

Essam Sharaf Prime minister of Egypt appointed by the Supreme Council of the Armed Forces (SCAF) during their time in power following Mubarak's demise. Thought to represent the revolution and said to be chosen by protesters in Tahrir, Sharaf quickly appeared subservient to the military's command and after a few short months came to be seen as weak and ineffectual, prompting protests calling for his removal.

Freedom and Justice Party The official political arm of the Muslim Brotherhood, the FJP is the umbrella party that serves as a platform for electoral purposes on behalf of the Brotherhood.

Goldstone The reference is to Richard Goldstone, the South African judge, international litigator, and investigator who led a fact-finding mission on the Israeli War on Gaza in 2008–2009.

Habib al-Adli Mubarak's longtime minister of interior, who presided over a period when the police committed crimes against political dissidents, including widespread torture in Egyptian prisons. Al-Adly became the target of activists' criticism prior to the January 25 protests in 2011.

Hamdeen Sabbahi Nasserist activist and journalist who ran in the first post-Mubarak presidential elections and came in third in the first round despite a weakly funded campaign. He later created and led the Popular Current, a leftist political party, and is a member of the National Salvation Front.

Hasan al-Banna A teacher and the first Supreme Guide of the Muslim Brotherhood. He founded the group in Egypt in 1928.

Hasan al-Ruwayni Military general and member of the Supreme Council of the Armed Forces (SCAF) during the transition period before the election of Muhammad Morsi. He is known for his problematic statements directed toward youth groups.

Hazim Abu Ismail Salafi cleric who gained widespread fame in the post-Mubarak era for his mobilization of supporters (known as "Hazemun") against SCAF, the Supreme Constitutional Court, the private media channels, and other groups. He also ran a high-profile presidential bid until he was disqualified because of his mother's naturalized American citizenship.

Hind al-Hinnawi Young Egyptian woman who rose to fame in 2005 when she went public as the mother of a child out of wedlock with a young actor, Ahmad al-Fishawi. Having broken a major taboo in Egyptian society, her case was the subject of widespread media attention.

Hisham al-Bastawisi Prominent judge and presidential candidate in the first post-Mubarak election.

Hisham Qandil First prime minister appointed by President Morsi.

Imam Prominent Egyptian footballing family that produced several top players over several generations.

Ismail Etman Military general and member of the Supreme Council of the Armed Forces (SCAF).

Al Jazeera A family of Qatar-based television stations that report on news from across the region and internationally. The Arabic station, set up in 1996, was once the most widely watched news network in the region and provided major coverage of the eighteen days of protest against Mubarak in 2011. Since the ascent of the Muslim Brotherhood, the network has lost much credibility inside Egypt for visibly favoring Islamist political groups over the opposition.

Kazibun campaign An activist campaign that aims to raise awareness about the misconduct of the military during the transition. Activists screen footage of violations by the military in public spaces across the country. The name means "Liars." A similar campaign, Ikhwan Kazibun (Brotherhood Liars), screens similar footage incriminating the ruling party.

Khairat al-Shater Prominent Muslim Brotherhood leader and member of the organization's Supreme Guide's Council. A wealthy entrepreneur, al-Shater is an influential figure in the Brotherhood's economic Nahda (Renaissance) program.

Khaled Ali Labor and human-rights lawyer who ran in the first presidential election after Mubarak.

Khaled Said Young Alexandrian man who was brutalized and killed by two police officers outside an Internet café in the summer of 2010. A Facebook page dedicated to him, entitled "We Are All Khaled Said," garnered significant support and called for the January 25, 2011 protests.

Mahalla labor incident The industrial city of Mahalla became the epicenter of labor-rights protests in 2008, leading up to a call for a general strike on April 6 of that year.

Mamdouh Shahin Prominent military general and member of the Supreme Council of the Armed Forces. Responsible for legal affairs, Shahin organized the constitutional declarations for the election processes throughout the eighteen months of military rule. He was also a member of the constituent assembly that drafted the constitution and ensured that the interests of the military establishment were preserved.

Maspero massacre On October 9, 2011, Coptic protesters converged on the state television building in Maspero, a section of Cairo. The military police guarding the building attacked protesters, leaving dozens dead and hundreds injured. Some protesters were shot with live ammunition and others run over by armored vehicles.

Maspero Youth Union A Coptic youth activism group that emerged after the toppling of Mubarak, demanding equal rights for Egypt's Christians and protesting attacks against the Coptic community across the country.

Mina Danial Young Christian socialist activist who was involved in the eighteen days of protest against Mubarak and then against the armed forces who ruled during the transition period. Danial was killed in the Maspero incident and became an iconic figure among Egypt's revolutionary youth.

Mo'az Muhammad Man from Dahshur who was killed in sectarian clashes in early August 2012 following an altercation over a burnt shirt at a Christian-owned laundry.

Mohamed ElBaradei Egyptian lawyer who served as the director of the International Atomic Energy Agency (IAEA) and won the Nobel Prize for Peace for his efforts to reduce nuclear proliferation. He became active in the Egyptian political environment following his retirement from the agency and was the first prominent international figure to challenge Mubarak's rule. He worked closely with youth in the country in a petition to amend the constitution to allow for an open presidential election and supported the January 25 protest and revolution from its outset. He is the head of the opposition National Salvation Front (NSF) and the founder of al-Dustur Party.

Mohamed El-Barghouthi Writer and columnist whose work is published in *al-Ahram* and *Al-Masry Al-Youm.*

Muhammad al-Assar A senior member of the Supreme Council of the Armed Forces (SCAF) and thought to be a central figure in the relationship between the Egyptian military and their American counterparts.

Muhammad Husayn Tantawi Mubarak's long-time minister of defense and the former head of the Supreme Council of the Armed Forces (SCAF). Field Marshal Tantawi was Egypt's de facto ruler during the eighteen months between the toppling of Mubarak and the election of Morsi.

Muhammad Mahmud battles Refers to a series of clashes between police forces and revolutionary youth on Muhammad Mahmud street, which is adjacent to Tahrir Square.

Muhammad Morsi The first elected president of Egypt after the fall of Mubarak. A prominent member of the Muslim Brotherhood's Supreme Guidance Council, Morsi was an elected parliamentarian during the Mubarak era and was chosen to lead the Brotherhood's Freedom and Justice Party (FJP) before becoming president.

Muhsin al-Fangari Military general and member of the Supreme Council of the Armed Forces (SCAF) who was the spokesperson for the authority during the transition period and became known for his brash and aggressive communication style.

Mustafa Bakry Prominent politician, journalist, and newspaper editor who espouses confusing and shifting views.

Mustafa Kamil (1874–1908) Prominent lawyer, journalist, and nationalist activist who founded the National Party in 1907, a few months before his death. The party has no relation to the National Democratic Party (NDP).

Nag' Hammadi shooting A drive-by shooting outside a church in the Upper Egyptian city of Nag' Hammadi on Coptic Christmas Eve, January 7, 2010, left nine dead and ten injured.

Naguib Sawiris An immensely successful businessman and entrepreneur with a net worth that makes him one of the world's richest people. With business dealings in construction, tourism, telecommunications, and television, Sawiris and his siblings are the most influential and visible Christian family in Egypt. Following the toppling of Mubarak, Sawiris became involved in politics, founding the liberal Free Egyptians Party.

National Democratic Party (NDP) Party founded by Anwar al-Sadat in 1978, committed to private enterprise and political centrism. The party's leadership was inherited by Hosni Mubarak following Sadat's assassination. During Mubarak's three decades of rule, the NDP became the only functional party as elections were monopolized and rigged. The party is often associated with widespread corruption, economic policies that favor the wealthy, and systematic abuse of human rights.

Nawal El Saadawy Perennial dissident feminist who began her career as a medical doctor in Egypt. The author of dozens of books, fiction and non-fiction, including *Woman at Point Zero* and *The Hidden Face of Eve,* El Saadawy is an ardent critic of the Mubarak regime, military rule, and political Islam.

al-Nour Party One of several political parties that represent the Salafi groups. With an agenda focused on the application of *sharia* law in Egypt, al-Nour scored significant gains in the first parliamentary elections after Mubarak. They were runners-up after the Muslim Brotherhood and secured around 25 percent of the seats in both houses of Parliament. They were also instrumental in the drafting of the polarizing Islamist-dominated constitution.

October 12 altercations in Tahrir Clashes between supporters and opponents of President Morsi occurred on this day in 2012, leaving over a hundred people injured.

Omar Suleiman The long-time head of Egypt's intelligence service under Mubarak, Suleiman came to be known for his close relationship to the United States and Israel. A mysterious military man with wide political influence, Suleiman was appointed Mubarak's vice president during the uprising, where he acted as the intermediary with the opposition. Although he shied away from the limelight, he will be remembered for reading Mubarak's short (thirty seconds) resignation message in a now-famous video. Suleiman continued to be an influential player during the SCAF-run transition and even submitted an application for candidacy in the presidential elections in a move widely thought to be a stunt. His sudden death on July 19, 2012 is considered by many to be suspicious.

Port Said massacre On February 1, 2012, following a football league match between al-Ahly and al-Masry in the city of Port Said, clashes ensued between supporters of the two teams, leaving over seventy dead and hundreds injured. It is widely believed that the violence was politically coordinated or facilitated to hit back at the Ultras (fanatical football fans) for their hostility towards the police and government.

Revolutionary Socialists A leftist revolutionary political group in Egypt focused on workers' rights and social justice.

Sa'd Zaghlul Fouad A polarizing yet obscure figure in Egyptian revolutionary history, Fouad was a fighter who was involved in attacks against the British colonial presence in Egypt before 1952, against Israel, and against any foreign involvement in the country.

Sayid Bilal Young Salafi man who was tortured to death in an Egyptian prison in Alexandria in conjunction with the bombing of the Two Saints Church on New Year's Eve in 2011. It is not clear whether Bilal had any connection to the incident; some argue that the attack was masterminded by the State Security Service and that Bilal was a scapegoat.

al-Sayyid Abd al-Aziz Head of the High Elections Commission.

Sharm al-Sheikh Resort city on the Red Sea coast, popular with divers and beach vacationers. It also became the site of a second home for Mubarak and his family toward the end of his rule.

Shaykh Wagdi Ghonim Radical Salafi cleric and Islamic scholar whose views are highly controversial. Banned for many years from traveling to Egypt, Ghonim maintains an active platform online filled with sermons and edicts that enjoy wide circulation.

Sidi Bishr Neighborhood in the Mediterranean city of Alexandria, site of the Two Saints Church bombing on January 1, 2011.

Suad Hosni Famous and much-loved Egyptian actress and entertainer who featured in many films in the 1970s and 1980s. Thought to have been coerced into working for one of the country's intelligence services, she died under suspicious circumstances in a fall from a balcony in London in 2001.

Tagammu' Party Leftist political party led by Tarek al-Said.

Tamim Al-Barghouti Palestinian-Egyptian poet and political scientist.

Tariq al-Bishri Senior judge and legal scholar who was consulted in the drafting of the constitutional declaration during SCAF's rule to determine the management of the country and the progress of elections. Thought to have Islamist leanings, al-Bishri has criticized the legal conduct of the both the military council and the Muslim Brotherhood.

Tawfiq Okasha Television personality who owned and ran the now-defunct station al-Fara'in, where he expressed eccentric and often incoherent views. Although he was not taken seriously politically, his ardent support for the military made him a favorite in the eyes of the ruling SCAF.

Two Saints Church bombing Bombing that occurred at the entrance of this Alexandrian church at midnight on New Year's Eve in 2011 as worshipers walked out. The attack left twenty-three dead and ninety-seven injured.

Ultras Groups of dedicated, fanatical football fans. Not unlike similar groups in Europe and South America, Ultras harbor enmity toward the police and are strongly critical of commercialized football. Ultras groups in Egypt were actively involved in the battles with the police during the eighteen days of the revolution and continue to be influential politically.

Umraniya incident In an attempt to prevent construction on a church property in the Umraniya neighborhood of Giza, police forces were deployed, leading to clashes with Coptic youth on November 24, 2010. The violence led to the death of one Christian demonstrator and dozens of injuries.

Wael Ghoneim Young Google executive who, with a group of others, initiated and administered the Facebook page dedicated to the memory of Khaled Said. Ghoneim has a wide following among Egyptian youth and has becoming a polarizing figure in the post-Mubarak era due to the increasingly divergent political atmosphere in the country.

Youssef Boutros Ghali Former minister of finance in Egypt under Mubarak. Now in exile in London, he faces charges of corruption during his time in office. He is considered one of the chief architects of Mubarak's neoliberal economic policy.

Zamalek Based in Cairo, Zamalek is the second most popular and successful Egyptian football club.

zibiba Arabic word for 'raisin,' the colloquial term used to describe a discoloration and scarring of the forehead caused by frequent prostration during prayer. It is often seen as a sign of religiosity.